SPEAKING DATA AND TELLING STORIES

DATE DUE

Speaking Data and Telling Stories examines the interdependent relationship between method (Data Verbalization) and practice (performance). Data Verbalization is about communicating and disseminating research data using performance approaches and techniques such as; spoken word, jazz, hip-hop, and reggae theatrics.

Martin Glynn calls for the development of performance-driven research dissemination that seeks to bring urgent attention to minority, excluded, and marginalized perspectives within research dissemination as a whole. Employing the data verbalization method creates an exciting new proposition that can give progressive researchers a unique and distinct voice, alongside generating significant reach and impact beyond the academy, conference, and peer reviewed journal.

The book will be an invaluable resource for researchers, scholars, and related practitioners who want to strengthen their ability to communicate and disseminate research data using live performance / spoken word approaches and techniques. It will also provide guidance for students and researchers wanting to generate wider environmental, social, and cultural impact using research data creatively.

Martin Glynn PhD is an internationally renowned criminologist, critical race scholar, theatre director, and dramatist. His research focuses on race and crime, black masculinities, and performance driven research dissemination.

SPEAKING DATA AND TELLING STORIES

Data Verbalization for Researchers

Martin Glynn

Routledge
Taylor & Francis Group

LONDON AND NEW YORK

First published 2019
by Routledge
2 Park Square, Milton Park, Abingdon, Oxon OX14 4RN

and by Routledge
52 Vanderbilt Avenue, New York, NY 10017

Routledge is an imprint of the Taylor & Francis Group, an informa business

British Library Cataloguing in Publication Data
A catalogue record for this book is available from the British Library

Library of Congress Cataloging-in-Publication Data
A catalog record has been requested for this book

ISBN: 978-1-138-48683-6 (hbk)
ISBN: 978-1-138-48684-3 (pbk)
ISBN: 978-1-351-04459-2 (ebk)

Typeset in Bembo
by Taylor & Francis Books

Printed and bound by CPI Group (UK) Ltd, Croydon, CR0 4YY

'Speaking Data and Telling Stories: Data Verbalization for Researchers' is dedicated in honour of my dear friend and colleague Dr Vinette 'Vinny' Cross. Vinette was a prominent and established researcher and academic who was constantly searching for ways to present her data in 'open, accessible, and inclusive' ways. She supported me unconditionally for over two decades and sadly passed away in October 2017. Her unwavering commitment, encouragement, and support for my vision to bring performance driven research data outside of the academy was the driving force behind 'data verbalization' that has remained with me till this day. This book will therefore continue to establish and build the kind of legacy that Vinny envisioned before her untimely passing. More importantly, I have pledged to work alongside other researchers, academics, educators, and practitioners, who are keen to see Data Verbalization as part of a wider continuum toward personal, social, and cultural 'change and transformation' using research data creatively which was always a core value of Vinny's work.

CONTENTS

TO MYSELF

The journey of this book from its inception to the actual publication has been a very humbling experience. In the past I've been critical of the work of some of my predecessors, not realising that all books are of their time and are not static in their claims. They are an extension of the researchers desire to create a legacy for their work. During my academic sojourn I have now acquired many new memories; collecting life stories, reading articles and books, discovering new and improved methods of disseminating research. Overall, this journey was a testing one, but one I needed to conclude. I'm now feeling a huge sense of relief regarding my lingering self-doubt as to whether 'data verbalization' will take its place in the continuum of research dissemination as a whole. I have pushed beyond the boundaries of that scared child hiding in the corner, to a child who wants to explore new things without living in fear of taking risks. Like an adrenalin rush new desires, thoughts, and feelings have pushed my curiosity to new heights. Mediocrity has no place in my life. Like a marathon runner I was poised to begin a long arduous journey where the route was mapped out, but my training had prepared me well. I am now more philosophical, gained new wisdom, and have acquired a mind not held captive by oppressive and dark forces. The need for validation has subsided, as accepting myself is more important than the emptiness of seeking the approval of others. The future may be uncertain and full of trepidation, but I'm relieved I have given myself permission to pursue my freedom.

ACKNOWLEDGEMENTS

I want to thank:

- My wife Jennifer, who was there at the beginning, is still here, and continues to be the emotional support that keeps me going at difficult times.
- Hannah Shakespeare at Routledge for commissioning me to write this book and realise a long-held dream.
- Anne Peaker, Professor's James Thompson, Johnny Saldana, and Norman Denzin, for providing me with the impetus to pursue my passion for integrating my passion for creative approaches to research dissemination.
- Richard Campbell (aka *so natural*) for his support and assistance in providing me with the music context for making 'data verbalization' accessible to the wider public.
- The doubters and the well poisoners who never thought I would get anywhere.
- Those silent voices who have inspired me to create something that will be able to assist researchers, artists, and practitioners finding common purpose by exploring performed 'counter narratives'.

DATA VERBALIZATION: SPEAKING DATA AND TELLING STORIES

As much contemporary research must now demonstrate significant social impacts
Research data dissemination must transcend the numbers 'N' move beyond mere facts
There is also a need to creatively distribute 'N' disseminate complex research data
That transcends the journal, the conference speech, 'N' moves it entirely off the paper
Presented in ways that are accessible, understood, inclusive, impacting 'N' engaging
Where the story of the data is taken from the initial idea, right thru to the staging
For critics 'N' detractors this is an epistemological 'N' ontological form of rehabilitation
Which is a dynamic oral rendition of research, known simply as 'data verbalization'

Data Verbalization is about communication, dissemination, 'N' robust interrogation
Of research data, that is a sensory, holistic, performative, a dramatic representation
Examining the interdependent relationship between practice 'N' inquiry that's critical
Presenting data that is three dimensional, analytical, physical, 'N' most of all lyrical
Explores difficult concepts, identifies emerging new patterns, paradigms, 'N' trends
Where biased assumptions about reliability 'N' validity are things you now have to suspend
Expanding the understanding of alternative methods of teaching, learning, 'N' assessment
Providing interactive ways to generate impact requires new forms of critical investment

Data Verbalization is about learning, developing new skills 'N' different ways to present
Appealing to audiences by inventing new forms of data distribution you must now invent
Presenting research findings to those who may be hard to access, identify, or reach.
Making complex ideas accessible, discovering new ways to educate, lecture 'N' to teach.
Communicating data for those who want change that is both meaningful 'N' productive
By establishing a culture of collaboration, interdisciplinary working, 'N' all things
inductive
At all times data should be put under scrutiny, with insightful reasoning 'N' investigation
Whilst creative reflexivity help you with your subjective biases 'N' personal fabrication

Data Verbalization is about delivering data creatively to gain 'N' reveal new insights
Deconstructing, reconstructing, taking the findings to new levels 'N' new heights
Communicating theoretical ideas 'N' paradigms by relocating them in a creative space
Presenting, consuming, 'N' understanding, issues of faith, gender, class, 'N' of course race

Constructing 'N' delivering teaching presented in non-conventional 'N' non-traditional ways
Making the complicated simple, the hidden visible, bringing clarity within the academic maze
Reworking the narrative, opening possibilities, exposing weaknesses 'N' all deep flaws
Where questions are raised to see what conclusions 'N' recommendations your data draws

Data Verbalization is about pedagogy 'N' producing new ways of interactive learning
Knowing that knowledge in itself is never static, but always twisting 'N' always turning
Where the numbers 'N' words are combined with music, visuals, movement, 'N' actions
Which present and represent themselves as numerous forms of dynamic interactions

Data Verbalization is about messages using three-dimensional research data promotion
Moving away from stoic peer review approval 'N' into the realms of feelings 'N' emotion
Where research outcomes wrestle with notions of communicating meaningful diversity
'N' creating a platform for data to go beyond the limitation 'N' confines of the university

Data Verbalization is about simplifying complex research themes, ideas, 'N' visions
Highlighting how policies, frameworks, laws, related issues, need clarity 'N' revisions
Revolutionising the way organisations can improve their communications literacy
Highlighting that progressive ways of sharing data by doing things non-traditionally
It is a critical response to exploring 'N' expressing the researcher's positionality
Alongside the ease of presenting research data with transparent functionality
Research participants can be part of the research process from beginning to end
Where concerns are observed, shared, 'N' solutions rise to the surface 'N' ascend

Data Verbalization should be critical, analytical, political, 'N' never ever be predictable
Should be metaphorical, allegorical, historical, 'N' occasionally sound rhetorical
Should be an adaptation 'N' a deconstruction of the original research that was factual
Presented in ways that are innovative, transformative, creative 'N' always practical
This new pathway for performing research data is an epistemological revolution
Where data verbalization present insights that will provide answers 'N' a new solution
It is dramatic, bold, defying traditional, conservative, 'N' biased research traditions
Where the researcher transcends their fears, anxieties, subordination 'N' personal inhibitions

Data Verbalization must guide inform, transform, 'N' shape, this voyage of discovery
By taking inaccessible research data thru' a process of resuscitation 'N' recovery
All research has to commit itself to investigating, discovering, 'N' find something new
Identifying different ways of seeing 'N' knowing from a completely different point of view
As much contemporary research must now demonstrate significant social impacts
Research data dissemination must transcend the numbers 'N' move beyond mere facts
There is also a need to creatively distribute 'N' disseminate complex research data
That transcends the journal, the conference speech, 'N' moves it entirely off the paper

WHO IS THIS BOOK FOR?

Speaking Data and Telling Stories: Data Verbalization for Researchers examines the interdependent relationship between 'method' (data verbalization) and 'practice' (performance). At a time when researchers are increasingly being called upon to demonstrate increased 'reach' and 'impact' in relation to their research, discovering fresh, innovative, and creative approaches to dissemination of important messages, ideas, and visions, contained within the data itself now becomes an important consideration. On researching the literature on research dissemination, I discovered a significant history in relation to 'data visualization'. Data visualisation is a technique that is widely used in both academic and corporate circles to present data in visual formats to explore and identify difficult concepts, emerging new patterns or complex connections contained within statistical data (Kirk, 2016). As a method, 'data visualisation' can give quantitative researchers a powerful platform from which to present their research in a 'visually literate' way. However, for qualitative researchers such as myself, there were a range of other considerations associated with disseminating research that required a frame of reference that fitted the context, orientation, and focus, of representing research that was complex, awkward, or controversial. I needed a breakthrough.

Breakthrough

Having read many books on research methods, I sadly discovered that scant attention had been paid to 'performance driven' approaches to research dissemination that involved the symbiotic relationship between 'spoken word', 'music', and 'storytelling'. On reflection, I acknowledged the legacy of progressive scholars past and present, inside and outside of the academy, who, at certain historical junctures, had wrestled with similar concerns as myself. Having operated as both an artist and researcher for many years I had always struggled to find appropriate spaces and outlets for disseminating my research both inside and outside the academy. Frustrated by this state of affairs I wanted to explore ways of presenting my research beyond the conference, workshop, and seminar circuit. So, I decided to position myself outside of peer review approval-validation and reconciled myself to facing the inner conflicts that surrounded my academic and scholarly identity. Namely, isolation and exclusion from so-called mainstream academia. I was further confronted with a significant personal truth. Namely, how could I 'speak to power', if the mechanism to do so (my research) had no voice. It was after much soul searching, further research, and an intensive development period, I brought the intersection of my work as a 'researcher', 'writer', and 'performer' together. This cumulative outcome laid the foundation for a method of disseminating research that I now refer to as 'data verbalization'.

> 'Data verbalization' is about 'communicating' & 'disseminating' research data using performance approaches & techniques.
>
> *(Glynn, 2016)*

I similarly knew that in order for me to progress beyond mere experimentation I had to commit myself to building on the works of my predecessors; Professor James Thompson (applied theatre), Professor Johnny Saldana (ethno-drama), and Professor Norman Denzin (performance auto-ethnography). Their works provided me with a continuum from which to build my ideas where they provided me with wise counsel throughout my journey. To them I owe a great deal of gratitude. On reading the works of Professor Saldaña further, communicating via email, alongside being featured in his book *Ethno-theatre* (Left Coast Press), I was blessed with further support from this great mentor. Professor Saldaña's words of encouragement were part of a longer sojourn around 'performance driven research dissemination'. Emerging out of the late '80s and early '90s working within the applied theatre movement under the mentorship of Professor James Thompson (Manchester University), I moved from representing the stories of black offenders using drama and performance, to tackling social/racial justice issues within criminal justice using performative ways of exploring the performed presentation of research. At that time, it didn't have a name, was raw, and felt more like 'experimentation with purpose' than a viable method. Although it would loosely be defined as applied theatre, my constant refining, questioning, and adaptation of ideas meant that there was no fixed definition that I could ascribe a suitable term. It was Professor Saldaña who later introduced me to 'ethno-drama' as a possible way forward, that acted as a suitable tipping point for my move into 'performance driven research dissemination'. It was the breakthrough I needed.

Ethnodrama

Ethnodrama consists of dramatized, significant selections of narrative collected through interviews, participant observation field notes, journal entries, and/or print and media artefacts, (Saldaña, 2005). Simply put, ethnodrama 'dramatizes research data'. The further justification for me using ethno-drama was rooted in what Green and Thorogood (2011) suggest, that policy makers have increasingly turned to qualitative methods of inquiry to enhance the understandings of how communities' function in relation to their own needs and concerns. Similarly, Denzin (2010) further suggests:

> At the beginning of a new century it is necessary to re-engage the promise of qualitative research as a 'radical democratic process'.
>
> *(2010: 6)*

At that time, I felt I had a possible vehicle from which to present the 'stories' of my research constituency in ways that could be observed, engaged, and interacted with. I also felt that ethno-dramatic representations could bring insight and understanding of marginalized communities to a new heightened prominence. I further felt that as ethno-drama started from an 'interpretivist' perspective that was both interactive and participatory it would further provide me with an ideal platform from which to explore the complexities of racial disproportionality within the criminal justice system. In some respect, at that time I embraced my 'activist scholarship' identity through my engagement with the performed representations of black offenders' 'counter-narratives' that forced me accept the work I was undertaking was now overtly political. In doing so ethno-drama enabled me to focus not just on the meanings that my research subjects gave to their lived experiences, but the resulting outcome laid the foundation for speaking racialized 'counter-narratives' (McAdams, 1985). The narrative potential of ethno-drama therefore offered me the possibility of restorying the past and reimagining the future. Over a period of many years I produced many ethno-drama's that were very successful and impacting, but the development process and resourcing proved to be problematic at times. However, I am eternally grateful to those who went before and hope that my humble contribution to research dissemination will honour, as well as extend, their legacy. My journey continued to push me forward, still not clear, but more of a radio frequency out of tune.

New journey

I was now in the era of populist politics, a proliferation of the far-right, Brexit, and a wider shift in the global economic situation. I needed to embrace new mediums such as social media platforms, on-line music distribution, alongside having to contend with the growth, proliferation of popular cultural word forms; hip-hop, grime, drill, and trap music that all had a major influence on the minds of young people. As much as the conservative side of me was still 'old school', I was a realist. Popular culture was here to stay. So, I had two ways to view this shift in the consciousness of society. Firstly, I could spend time opposing the negative portrayal and impact that some of these outputs were having on the wider society, or secondly, I could embrace these mediums and plant a different message in the hearts and minds of young people, and in turn, the wider community using those same mediums. My logic was rooted in the understanding that if social media platforms are so powerful promoting 'anti-social' messages, then I can use my own research on those same platforms by presenting 'pro-social' messages. I reflected deeply on the situation and decided I needed something that was more immediate than ethno-drama, not held back by moral gate keepers, as well as being accessible to the wider community. I further knew that I wanted to create something that would have the immediacy of popular music, the potency of theatre, and a simplicity of understanding; that I christened 'learning on the go'. 'Learning on the go' was about supplying a demand for my research using those mediums that could be accessed through headphones; music, podcasts, live recordings, etc. The context for 'data verbalization' was now set. The ultimate vision and mission therefore was to take my research, adapt it using a mixture of 'storytelling' expressed through 'performance' using a combination of 'spoken word' and 'music', distributing the outcomes on social media platforms. So here it was, I had forged a new frontier, where my research could now 'be spoken', while at the same time, 'tell a story'. The underpinning aspect of my vision was to unapologetically appeal to the 'academic in the artist' and the 'artist in the academic'. With this in mind, I envisioned 'data verbalization' would become part of a wider personal legacy designed to move research dissemination outside of the academy and into the communities where the research was co-produced. It was against this backdrop that the genesis for my book *Speaking Data and Telling Stories: Data Verbalization for Researchers* was born. For researchers keen to embrace data verbalization as a method of disseminating research a range of potential pedagogical features offer some interesting new possibilities such as:

- **Knowledge exchange:** Covers the processes by which new knowledge is co-produced between academic, non-academic individuals and communities working in partnership.
- **Public engagement:** An umbrella term for any activity that engages the public with research and involves reciprocated interaction, collaboration and partnership.
- **Performance reflexivity:** Involves exploring and examining the researcher's conceptual baggage; assumptions and biases in relation to research decisions.
- **Pedagogy:** To develop new ways of teaching, delivering lectures, seminars, and workshops in a diverse range of settings; traditional, non-traditional, site specific, flipped-blended learning, etc.
- **Key message promotion:** Important messages/themes contained within research reports can be adapted into a 'performative' context, making the outcomes accessible and inclusive to a wide and diverse audiences.
- **Organisational visioning:** A process of developing consensus about what the organisation wants, and then deciding what is necessary to achieve it. Using an approach that is 'performative' can revolutionise the way organisations develop strategic frameworks by enhancing and improving their overall approach to 'communications literacy'

It is my further contention that 'data verbalization' can give all researchers a unique and distinct platform from which to generate significant reach and impact, beyond the academy, conference, and peer review journal. In essence 'data verbalization' aims to take its place within the wider research dissemination community as a whole. If what I've set out connects to your own sense of curiosity, then this book is for you. Whereas ethnodrama 'dramatizes the data', data verbalization 'speaks the data'. Please walk with me.

Martin Glynn (2019)

ORGANISATION OF THE BOOK

Chapter One: Hearing the subtext

This chapter calls for a revision of the use of creative approaches to 'research dissemination'. I come to this position based on having used storytelling, poetry, theatre, and film in a variety of contexts and situations; education, public health, criminal justice, and youth work, for most of my working life. During this period, I have had many requests for my techniques, methods, and approaches, to be made available for use in; training sessions; professional development workshops; group work activities; lecturing, etc. As a dramatist I have also been fortunate to have had many of my ideas produced for the stage, screen, radio, and lately social media. Similarly, as an academic I have used an intersection of my academic-creative skills to provide a platform for many 'silent' and 'invisible' research participants voices to speak to the world. It is therefore the focus of this introductory chapter to envision more contemporary ways for the 'sub-textual' elements of research to be seen, heard, and experienced.

Chapter Two: Performing research and praxis

This chapter explores 'data verbalization' and its potential reach in assisting 'praxis'. It builds on the work of Brazilian Augusto Boal who was in sympathy with oppressed people and believed in their ability to change using theatre as the conduit. Boal (1993) further encouraged critical thought about oppressive social conditions and developed 'theatre of the oppressed' where he believed that 'praxis' could be actualized using creative means such as theatre. In my work in prisons I too have sought numerous ways to engage offenders in (creative) transformative processes that would aid their rehabilitative and desistance trajectories. It was during my doctoral research that I was given invaluable advice by eminent sociologist Howard Becker who pushed me to look critically at the role of performing research as a contributory aspect of assisting in the actualisation of praxis. Howard encouraged me to use a creative approach when advocating around issues associated with criminal, social, and racial justice issues. He further urged me to 'persuade' my critics, 'convince' the sceptics, 'empower' those I engage with, and to 'transform' the lives of oppressed, marginalized, and disaffected communities by using non-traditional approaches to critical inquiry. This chapter concludes with envisioning a framework designed to assist researchers in transcending the current peer review system, connected to the wider agendas of social and racial justice using 'data verbalization'.

Chapter Three: Data verbalization and bricolage

This chapter argues for the need to engage researchers in a critical dialogue that moves beyond the confines of academic silos applying a 'bricolage' approach to performance driven research dissemination. The French word 'bricoleur' describes a handyman or handywoman who makes use of the tools available to complete a task. Bricolage research in essence means unifying multiple qualitative research approaches. By integrating different research paradigms, it is hoped new understandings will emerge and reframe an agenda that is badly in need of an overhaul. Denzin and Lincoln (2000) argue that researchers employing the use of bricolage approach must not strive for neutrality but instead acknowledge subjectivity within the research process itself. The employment of the use of 'bricolage research' extends the possibility of research impacting at the level of social and racial justice. Important here is in the understandings of the researcher's positionality and reflexive accounts within the research domain. This chapter therefore proposes that 'bricolage' research could provide a way forward. Although 'bricolage', as an approach to qualitative inquiry, has gained popularity in academic circles, it remains relatively misunderstood, and unpopular, in broader research communities. It is hoped that 'data verbalization' becomes a welcome addition to the bricolage canon of ideas.

Chapter Four: Creating and producing data verbalization

This chapter introduces the conceptual thinking behind 'data verbalization'. 'Data verbalization' is about 'communicating' & 'disseminating' research data using performance approaches & techniques (Glynn, 2016). It looks at the various stages and processes associated with producing 'data verbalization':

- Extracting the story from the data
- Audience development
- Method of verbalizing (speaking) research data
- Producing and staging data verbalization

It concludes by looking at the interdependent relationship between method (data verbalization) and practice (performance).

Chapter Five: Data verbalization and impact

This chapter focuses on the contentious issue of 'reach' versus 'impact'. As universities are under increasing pressure to generate research, impact 'data verbalization' offers a proposition on increasing both reach and impact by bringing performed 'counter narratives to the attention of the wider public and global audiences. Whereas peer review articles and textbooks generate a small readership, my first data verbalization story found a significant presence on social media platforms (reach), bringing my research to an international audience. This chapter concludes by arguing that data verbalization can move research data into communities much the same as Freirean 'participatory research' and Boalian 'theatre of the oppressed' have done.

Chapter Six: Data verbalization and the presentation of self

This chapter looks at 'performance auto-ethnography' as part of an enhanced research dissemination strategy for researchers. Auto-ethnography is about finding strategies to question the researcher's attitudes, thought processes, values, assumptions, prejudices, and habitual actions within the research trajectory. A reflexive-minded researcher is a stronger proposition than someone who merely undertakes reflection as practical problem-solving. It is my view that 'performance reflexivity' can assist the researcher, research participants, and constituent communities outside of the academy in drawing understanding, insights, and challenges faced by the researcher when conducting the research itself. Performance reflexivity therefore can further develop a bonded relationship where the researcher becomes a 'trusted other' as an essential part of building confidence within the researcher's own constituency. This chapter concludes by arguing that performance reflexivity not only validates the researcher's role, but more importantly serves as an integral, not separate, element of the research enquiry itself.

Chapter Seven: Blended learning and data verbalization

This chapter focuses on 'data verbalization' as a complimentary method that can work alongside 'blended learning'. Blended learning is a pedagogical approach in which direct instruction moves from the group learning space to the individual learning space, which becomes part of the creation of a transformative, dynamic, and interactive learning environment. In today's media-driven world dominated by music, digital platforms, screen, and headphone culture, data verbalization offers the possibility of engaging with a 'learning on the go' pedagogy. This chapter concludes by exploring the consequences and implications of deploying such as approach in relation to blended learning as a whole.

Chapter Eight: Data verbalization and social media

This chapter calls for dissident scholarship, to challenge conventional understandings and accepted boundaries with relation to how research is disseminated.

Some scholars argue that no one method can adequately lay claim to holding the answers of the complex nature of how research can impact in the lives of real people based on a lack of unification among academic disciplines. It is therefore incumbent on all researchers to transcend straightforward explanations and neat theoretical understandings pertaining to research and occupy space outside of the comfort zone of the 'ivory tower'. Moving toward a more 'mediated imagination' requires updated and technologically relevant methods. This chapter posits that there are new debates that now need to be had, consequences and concerns that need to be raised, and contemporary understandings must be addressed in line within the society in which we live. It further calls for the researcher not to abandon traditional ways of disseminating research, but to seize this moment in history that will preserve the past in a virtual space.

Epilogue: Future directions

This chapter concludes the book with arguing for the need to develop an improved and more appropriate theoretical lens from which to disseminate research data. Intersectionality as Crenshaw (1999) argues is the understanding that human beings are shaped by the interaction of their different social locations which occur within a context of connected systems and structures of power. It envisions the use of this new theoretical lens operating as a counter narrative designed to contest and challenge dominant and oppressive research paradigms. Counter-narratives are important as they use collective stories as a way of contesting the dominant narratives of those who oppress. Bell (2003) argues that future research should move beyond merely descriptive accounts of oppression. Bell further sees the need to address how multiple inequalities influence outcomes for marginalised populations. The 'intersectional nature of 'data verbalization' may enable communities to narrate, to interpret events, and to bring coherence to how they see their own concerns (McAdams, 1985). In doing so this chapter concludes the book by presenting a 'data verbalization' manifesto designed to improve the engagement with, and connection to, wider public and social policy concerns, while at the same time shaping how those policies are designed and delivered.

References

Bell, D. (2003) 'Telling tales: what stories can teach us about racism', *Race, Ethnicity and Education*, 6(1): 3–28.
Boal, A. (1993) *Games for Actors and Non-Actors*, London: Routledge.
Crenshaw, K. (1999) 'Mapping the margins: intersectionality, identity politics and violence against women of color', *Stanford Law Review*, 43: 1241–1299.
Denzin, N.K. (2010) *The Qualitative Manifesto*, Walnut Creek: Left Coast Press.

Denzin, N.K., & Lincoln, Y. (2000). *Handbook of Qualitative Research* (2nd ed.), Thousand Oaks, CA: Sage.

Glynn, M. (2016) 'Platform "Data Verbalization Lab" Creative Dissemination of Research Data', *Journal to the Stage (Project Report)*, Birmingham: Birmingham City University.

Green, J. and Thorogood, N. (2004) *Qualitative Methods for Health Research*, London: Sage.

Kirk, A. (2016) *Data Visualisation: A Handbook for Data Driven Design*, London: Sage.

McAdams, D. (1985) *Power, Intimacy, and the Life Story*, London: Guildford Press.

Saldaña, J. (Ed.). (2005). *Ethnodrama: An Anthology of Reality Theatre*, Walnut Creek, CA: AltaMira Press.

PROLOGUE

To be or not to be Data Verbalization?

In 2016, I was given a small development grant from Birmingham City University to pilot the 'data verbalization lab'; a space for colleagues, students, and community members interested in experimenting with research data. On conclusion of the course I was approached by (one of the attendees), Birmingham-based music producer Richard Campbell (aka Natural and Secret), to work in partnership with a view to creatively adapting my research. The outcome resulted in the production of 'Silenced', a jazz hip-hop fusion that became the first 'data verbalization' story. Important here, was the adaptation brought significant new attention to my original research as it was widely distributed on several social media platforms and digital music radio programmes. This outcome further pushed the boundaries of my approach to 'performance driven research dissemination' and brought it to a new heightened prominence. However, a range of issues now emerged.

Conflicted

As I wrestled with yet another institutional edict trying to define, control, and direct what constituted notions of my research 'impact' and 'reach', I grew tired of the biased thinking and negative assumptions that attempted to define and control what the parameters of my research should be, how it should be measured, and more importantly how it should be disseminated. So, I took a pragmatic decision. Namely, any future trajectory of my research would not be watered down or subjected to unfair 'institutional expectations' or elitist 'peer review protocols'. I knew I had to confront the resistance of the so-called 'traditionalists'; those individuals who saw my experimentation around research dissemination as the basis for asserting an academic exclusion zone designed to prolong my scholarly marginalization. Symbolically, it felt like I was being treated this way for no other reason than it posed a threat to the natural order that traditionally excluded creative approaches to research dissemination.

Status quo

By not upholding the status quo, many of my colleagues rendered the public acknowledgement of my research invisible, obsolete, and dismissed it as not worthy of attention. Having had a lived experience where historically, politically, culturally, and socially, I had been marginalized as a person of colour, I was not going to sit back and watch the same mind-set relegate my research to the bargain basement. So, I continued to adapt my research and presented it back to my co constructors. Again, the silences from some of my academic colleagues continued to be deafening. After several exhausting years of being ignored, blanked out, and consigned to the margins, I moved beyond the development phase of 'data verbalization' where I began to 'speak' my research, merged with my other passion, 'music'. Suddenly, the reception in my numerous research constituencies and communities I had worked with was overwhelming. Appreciation from around the world gathered momentum, a book deal from a major publisher (Routledge) came to fruition, combined with a rush of inquiries from progressive academics, agencies, and practitioners followed. Yet again, throughout all of this period there was still a 'tumbleweed silence' coming from some quarters of the so-called 'mainstream' academic world, peer review journals, and academic silos. Inasmuch that I now felt that 'speaking research' was seen in certain academic circles as weakening the genetic make-up of so-called traditional 'data dissemination' that languishes privately between the pages of academic journals, conference halls, and talk shops. It was at this point I had come to terms with this state of affairs. In my naïve period as an early career researcher I believed that there was a space for me in academia, but I was wrong. The relentless colonisation within academia of the neo-liberalist agenda crept up slowly and became a fierce adversary who refused to back down when challenged. It was to this end I took some conscious decisions about my future is academia with relation to positionality, bias, and exclusivity;

- **Positionality** – I accepted that my researcher positionality further undermined any notion of objectivity I may have had, and in doing so I risked losing any significant reliability and validation of my work within so called 'mainstream' academia.
- **Bias** – In spite of the power and sheer impact of music, it is still seen as secondary to positivistic elements within our society where science is seen as more important than the 'soul' and how one feels. This bias mean that validation would have to be sought elsewhere.
- **Exclusivity** – The desire to see my research as a tool for liberation and transformation clashed with conservative ideals regarding research dissemination where objectivity in research superseded the nature of 'subjective inclusivity'.

At times it was disconcerting not to be invited to the party, while at the same time seeing other researcher's progress profiled because they fitted the bill.

However, as my integrity and self-worth were the core values that underpinned who I was as a person, it all became clearer. I harboured no malice toward my detractors, nor did I desire to be part of an exclusive club that couched authenticity in arrogance and pretence. As 'data verbalization' grew and armed progressive researchers with the tools they needed to advance their ideas outside of academia, I found a place of solace, comfort, and calm. In essence, my future direction was less of an external expression of self, but more a journey of the soul. By bringing together my love of research and music for the greater good, I was now at peace with the contribution I had made to the 'production of knowledge'. Much the same as a composer or playwright, my inner need to tell excluded stories, present counter-narratives, and to speak to power, meant having to accept that I was now an active and political scholar who wanted to use research for 'emancipatory' purposes.

Transition point

I also accepted that my journey as a researcher was nothing more than a transitional point on my own continuum as a concerned member of society who saw making 'power and authority' accountable to those who are impacted by biased and oppressive research. 'Data verbalization' therefore was, and still is, an extension of a long tradition of researchers, scholars, and creative artists, trying to maintain the continuity of research dissemination relevant for a changing world, even if the problems remain within a constant socio-historical context. Data verbalization's future vision therefore aims to locate the 'speaking of research' within a global context. In doing so it hopes to bring 'performance driven' research into a space that moves beyond the confines of academia. Equally as important is to equip researchers, educators, practitioners, and other related professionals with the tools to turn 'data into action', that will lead to wider social and cultural impacts. A point of note, this book is not a definitive guide to research dissemination. This book is a 'speculative text' that requires further work, experimentation, and development. However, it is an attempt to provide researchers, practitioners, and communities with some tools to assist in the promotion of ideas that get left behind, are seldom published, or are side-lined because they don't suit the current neo-liberal agenda. So here I am, not at a crossroads, stuck in an abyss, or begging to be let into to a locked room. I have discovered, like many slaves, freedom is a price work paying. So please walk with me. Join me in this intellectual and creative sojourn through the landscape of 'data verbalization'.

Summary

This chapter was a personal reflection of some of my thoughts leading up to the development of the book. The need to underpin the overall structure in this was predicated by a deeper need to reveal that my core motivation was an intersection of the personal and political. In doing so I am positioning myself as both a creative-active scholar, where there is a symbiotic relationship between everything I do as a researcher. This introductory prologue is therefore a rallying cry to any researcher reading this book who are dissatisfied with the apolitical stance of much contemporary research.

Reflective questions

1. What is your own positionality with relation to your research and its dissemination?
2. What does your position reveal about you and your researcher trajectory?
3. What kind of strategy do you have in place to embrace the intersection of the personal and political within your research?

1

HEARING THE SUBTEXT

This chapter lays the foundation for data verbalization as a contemporary 'performance driven research dissemination' method-technique. It further calls for a revision of research dissemination practices and approaches as a whole. I come to this position as stated previously, based on a history of denied access, exclusion, and marginalization from so-called mainstream academic circles. It is my firm belief that in a techno-centred society, research should 'speak to power' using mediums that gives voice to legitimate concerns from powerless and disadvantaged communities working along-side progressive researchers committed to social justice goals. For most of my working life I have used storytelling, poetry, theatre, and film in a variety of contexts and situations; education, public health, criminal justice, and youth work. During this period, I have had many requests for my techniques, methods, and approaches, to be made available for use in; training sessions, professional development workshops, group work activities, lecturing, etc. As a dramatist I have also been fortunate to have had many of my ideas produced for the stage, screen, and radio. Similarly, as an academic I have used an intersection of my academic-creative skills to provide a platform for many 'silent' and 'invisible' participants voices to speak to the world on their own terms. It is therefore a key focus of this introductory chapter to envision a way for research to be heard by 'speaking the data', (data verbalization). To do so I want to share my own personal journey as a way of contextualising 'data verbalization' as a reflexive account of my ongoing academic identity.

My journey

Friday 7 March 2014 was my PhD graduation day, which heralded the end of an arduous academic journey and the beginning of a new phase of my researcher identity as I was now officially acknowledged as an 'academic'. Not just any academic I might add, but someone from an inner-city background, who was non-white, and in his late 50s. The immediacy of the intersectional nature of my identity had suddenly found new purpose. Although I didn't know it at the time, the battle scars of my time as a doctoral student needed some much-needed attention and more importantly, healing. If the truth be told I'd never really sat comfortably (still don't) within the confines of the so-called 'ivory tower' as I felt the constant pressure of having to conform to academic norms that at times tried to subordinate any sense of authenticity I had as an academic who was both racialized as black and critical. At times when I did assert a sense of cultural or racial pride, it was dismissed, labelled, and stigmatized. I did not feel connected to the growth and proliferation of the emerging 'black bourgeoisie' I encountered in the academy who tried to convince me that 'moderated blackness', would somehow give me credibility and tenure alongside the 'white elite' that many of them tried to emulate. Although at times it felt I was languishing in a black–white binary, I somehow knew it was a transitory moment. My overall desire was to be free from the 'plantation mentality' that drove a lot of my colleagues toward a mental decline based on having to navigating the 'white space of academia' that depleted both my emotional and physical energy and impacted significantly on any notion of positive psychic preservation. For me this was a period of personal reflection. One of the most rewarding aspects about being in mid-life is in the capacity to be straight with myself. My children were now grown and living independent lives, my grandchildren gave me a reason for telling tall stories, and I could at last feel comfortable at giving less energy to the dictates of anyone or anything that got in the way of my transition into this new phase of my life.

Clarity

Clarity about 'who' not 'what' I was bounded into my consciousness and brought me to a new point of personal understanding, which was more empowering than wallowing in the angst-ridden midlife crisis that was, and still is, ever present in my life. Don't get me wrong there were, and still are, moments where self-doubt and over-analysing things crept into my consciousness that usually results in me sitting down and writing things out my system, more than festering alone with my thoughts. My life was now full of new thoughts, desires, and more importantly dreams. For the cynics among you I hadn't won the lottery, nor had I paid the mortgage off, and I certainly was not flying high on the adrenalin of being in mid-life. Like many men, I had found being in mid-life hard, debilitating at times, and for the most part isolating, on account of the combination of physical and emotional changes taking place internally. So, I decided it was time to take stock take of my life. Physically, things could have been better, and my internal workings were calling out for a much-needed shift away from the treadmill existence that has been a staple of my life for many years.

New horizons

I remembered being at the start of a new semester when I announced to a new group of students that I was considering retirement. Yes! I had decided that after 35 years of frontline criminal justice practice, as many years lecturing, combined with the disillusionment of life 'post doctorally' I needed to move on with my life. I wanted to be free to change direction, seek new challenges, and more importantly do something for me. Unlike many of my colleagues I had developed new interests outside of the academy, where my doctorate was merely a tool to assist me in those pursuits. Plus, I had got married (aged 61). However, constantly hearing student's questioning about my own positionality made me pause for a moment of critical reflection. My insecurities notwithstanding, the anticipation of new personal growth superseded any fears I might have had. In spite of some strong lingering doubts and being fearful of the consequences of pursuing a new and unfamiliar road, the mask of excitement slipped off as I felt a huge emptiness engulf me like a dense fog. I knew I didn't want to continue going through the motions of my current liminal academic existence even if it was comforting as the desire and craving for a new adventure was more dominant. I then retreated to the safety and comfort of my vast array of books hoping they would come to my aid with an answer to my plight. I glanced around at my trusted friends and felt something good was going to happen. They brought the ancestral spirits to the fore and provided me with much-needed guidance and wisdom. Today felt like a different moment, a transitional one.

Reconnection

My eyes moved from side to side, up and down. Like soldiers on parade out they stepped. I pulled out four books; W.E.B. Du Bois (1938) *Souls of Black Folk*, Amiri Baraka (1963) (Formerly Leroi Jones) *Blues People*, Manning Marable's (1995) *Beyond Black and White*, and finally, Arthur Bochner's (2014) *Coming to Narrative*. I quickly removed them from the shelves and relocated to the living room, where I reacquainted myself with them, like old friends who hadn't seen each other in a long time. I scanned the pages voraciously, familiarizing myself with our previous encounters. I was on a mission. And then the penny dropped. Each book different in style, tone, and content, were not academic journal articles, but more of a series of essays written from both personal and intellectual standpoints. DuBois's notion of 'Double Consciousness' reminded me of the time I found myself adrift in academia. Amiri Baraka's acerbic tones on the other hand wrote with a passionate anger about racism in 1960s America, that helped me contextualize the contemporary reality of being black and academic, within a predominantly white institution. Manning Marable's essays similarly made me feel comfortable with the importance of not separating my public, professional, and personal self, from the politics of racialization and blackness. And finally, Arthur Bochner reminded me that the reconciliation of my divided self, transcended the need for academic validation.

Relief

Moments later I shed a few tears of relief, followed by dousing myself in John Coltrane's 'Love Supreme'. I now had what I needed to proceed to the next level. A decision that would change the direction of my academic future. Excited by my discovery I went to see my wife Jen. I told her that their writing had pushed me to find a way to be the kind of academic I wanted to be. The kind of academic that embraced passion, not the security of tenure, a research contract, or a senior lecturer's position. I no longer felt the insecurity of indecision. I went back to my computer, dredged my files, and discovered to my surprise that I had written many essays, journal articles, and scripts. I felt it was time to bring them to life. I took the decision there and then to dedicate myself to put my academic work into a creative form and reconnect to my formers passions. I now had to confront a deeper issue. Namely, the choice not to retire, but to reposition myself within the wider academic landscape that had previously excluded me. I now wanted to push the boundaries of negative conservative academic expectations to dedicate myself to 'adapting' and 'performing' my research and build a new future for myself; less as a traditional academic, but more of a 'performance driven dissemination specialist'.

Safe space

I wanted to occupy a new 'safe space' where intellectual subjectivity would not be a barrier to me exploring what I felt about the things in my research that concerned me and were most important to the wider community. For years I'd felt uneasy at sending my stuff to academic journals knowing that some of my peers may read what I'd been doing, but the community from which my work had emerged would never see or read them. Equally as upsetting was the countless conferences I'd spoken at, where hardly anyone looked like the participants of my research. I remembered how many hours I'd spent alone in hotel rooms after the conference sessions had finished wondering if I had any impact, or if I just being scoped out by the competition of other competitive academics vying for a place in the academic Olympics. This state of affairs has always troubled me, and still does. Mainly because I am a critical researcher, criminologist, dramatist, and a community person from the inner city who seldom sees the implementation of the recommendations many of us push out in our reports and articles. The continuous observations of the crumbling inner city infrastructure where I live, combined with the lack of resources available to repair the broken human dam for me, demanded a response.

My divided self

As a criminologist I had been steeped in the outgrowths of human misery where a life can be lost easily through crime and violence, where young people are no longer seeking mediation to solve disputes, and the duality of 'moral panic' and the 'fear society' reduce notions of 'community' to a mere sound bite in the local media. As a parent, grandparent, and lately, a great-grand parent I had similarly seen my idealism around notions of family and community replaced with generations facing more social disorganization than social cohesion. For years I had also encountered so many 'shadow people'; those silent voices on the margins of society who demanded that I bring their stories to a wider public. Reflecting on Bochner's view of the 'divided self' I decided that I could no longer subscribe to living with my 'divided self' for the sake of appeasing the liberal consciousness of academics both black and white. I also lacked interest in gaining credibility inside academia that had declared war on the articulation of anything that wants to contest both the epistemological and ontological claims supporting 'white privilege' that rendered my difference/s subordinate.

Post-doctorally

Then it happened. A unification of my 'divided self' provided both the stimulus and tipping point by bringing a much-needed truce to my personal and professional personas. For the first time in years they were no longer at war with each other. It was my intellectual coming of age, with the pulse of a hip-hop beat, the fire of a reggae bass-line, and the power of a Coltrane solo. More importantly my thoughts, feelings, and ideas now saw the light of day. However, in spite of the knowledge I now possessed, I still struggled with knowing that few things had changed in the world of the criminal justice system since completing my doctorate. When I look back, I was in a state of denial for quite some time during the early stages of my academic career post-doctorally. Namely, the primary goal of researchers like me is to shape the consciousness of the disaffected, marginalized, and those lingering in the shadows, and to equip with them with the tools so they can seek their liberation. In essence the lesson discovered here was my studies, the pursuit of new knowledge, and the pain of academic study, was no longer about my own personal brand of selfishness, but one that was part of a 'cycle of change' where I was a mere cog in a bigger wheel. I decided I needed to remove of my negative thinking and pursue my own truth.

Breaking free

I knew that I had to break free from the narrow academic constructs, where the ideals of power, privilege and elitism remained heavily embedded within the dominant culture within the institution. I needed to (re)define my academic identity by engaging in a more mature conversation about my scholarly positionality. I believed that scholars like myself must look outward and consider the changing realities of living in a modern society. To this end I decided I did not want to replicate structures and frameworks that excluded on the basis of placing academic status in a vanguard position, above the marginalized and disaffected communities that informed my research portfolio. Having been engaged in many research and evaluations I became increasingly concerned about the restrictions, barriers, and difficulties in bringing my work to the attention of the public, commissioners, policy makers, etc. I was equally as concerned that when my work was presented, the academic conventions that were available stipulated that I presented my findings in ways that at times did not do justice to the 'voices' and 'stories' of the participants, who were the co-constructors of my research, who shared their testimonies with me throughout the research process. Coming from a performance background I had always operated outside the box by finding creative ways to bring the key messages to my audience in accessible ways.

Continuing struggle

However, I had struggled to find any significant infrastructure, training programmes, or learning modules that would assist others in wanting to combine research and performance as a way of creating an innovative way of disseminating their work. Recently, old friends and contacts from my past reminded me that I was always a storyteller who influenced others through the power of story. My ability to tell 'lies' as a child through fabricating and bending the truth, combined with holding an audience captive, reminded me that the foundation for my current journey was laid a long time ago. Having worked in hundreds of schools running creative writing/performance workshops, undertaken countless residencies in criminal justice, public health, and educational settings, combined with delivering conference speeches, and conducting research projects, it was evident that the capacity to communicate my ideas has by and large been transmitted through stories. Some of it has been performative, while others have been philosophical, and lately with my academic work I have had to use stories to break down complex and sophisticated abstract ideas contained within my research. The acknowledgement that stories important and can impact on many different levels is important here.

Story-making

Using storytelling to inspire, motivate, and uplift; whether at school, in the community, in a prison, or any other spaces I found myself in, telling stories enabled them to work through problems using the 'story wisdom' I imparted. As modern living is at times fraught with complex, difficult, and confusing challenges there is a need to re-establish a series of guiding principles and truths by which we can reframe our hectic lives. Stories are about individual and collective memory that helps shape, define, and understand our personal or collective meaning and purpose. Stories bind people together and allow each individual to better comprehend their place in the world. Storytelling therefore is an ideal conduit for accessing 'handed down' and 'passed on' wisdom that can be used as part of a process of personal development, transformation, and more importantly 'leadership'. Storytelling is an ancient art. People used to tell stories around camp fires or paint them on cave walls. Stories were passed down the generations by memory and word of mouth. Later, people would write stories into books and represent them in paintings and sculptures and even perform them in theatres. More recently stories were made into films and shown in cinemas. Nowadays these stories are screened on television and computer screens. While technologies have only been around for a few years, the types of stories that are told on them have existed for as long as humanity has had language. Stories are the way we communicate our myths (our explanations of the world, how it began and why it is how it is). Stories help us to understand our own lives better by presenting and discussing the lives and experiences of others. They engage us by taking us out of our everyday lives into imaginary worlds that move, inform, and entertain us as a way to assist others on their journey of discovery, in developing effective leadership through the acquisition of storytelling wisdom. To move research from the 'page to the stage' created significant scope, opportunities, and possibilities to not only push the boundaries of current thinking, but to envision a new landscape where research brings the type of changes that would impact on both the human condition, communities, and society in equal measure. This made me think more critically about the need for performed 'counter narratives'.

The need for counter narratives

Denzin and Giardana (2017) argue that teachers, researchers, and public servants, of all traditions are uniquely equipped to take up the charge, to reach beyond the walls of the profession, to engage with disparate and competing publics, to conduct research that materially effects if not changes the course of historical present. Denzin (2010) similarly calls for each generation to articulate its epistemological, methodological, and ethical stance toward critical inquiry. Mills (1959) also sees the challenge is to develop methodologies that allow us to examine how the private troubles of individuals are connected to public issues and to public responses to these troubles. Brown and Strega (2005) likewise express the view that traditional approaches to research must also strive to capture and legitimize alternate ways of knowing. Denzin (2018) so too believes that lives, experiences, the telling, and the told are represented in stories which are performance based. In my experience many researchers who do not engage with or understand the role of 'story' or 'storying' research, limits the possibilities for research to be utilized as part of the wider pursuit of social justice. Stories, like pictures that have been painted over, and, where paint is scraped off as an old picture, can create something new and become visible. Research for me should always strive to reflect the words and narratives of the 'speaker/s' and 'knower/s' of their truths, as they attempt to give meaning and shape to the lives they lead. Stories, then, are always open ended, never finished, ambiguous, and subject to multiple interpretations. Ellingson (2017) reaffirms my own belief that research should depend upon participatory approaches to shared power with participants equally. Sharing power should enable research subjects to be less restricted by the power and control of the researchers' academic credentials. The emphasis should be rooted in the value of the research subject's perspectives and knowledge, grounded in their everyday lives. This further pushes me to argue for the need of a revision in terms research dissemination that is rooted in story and creativity, expressed through performance.

Revision

The need for a revision should be driven by a principled ethical stance where research should serve the communities in which it is conducted;

> Knowledge emerges through narrative when it is used strategically and con-
> nected in an ongoing dialogic between 'telling' and 'doing', between narra-
> tive, reflection, and praxis.
>
> *(Ritchie & Wilson, 2000: 172)*

Engaging in an ongoing conversation that turns storytelling into pedagogy may
provide the subjects of our research with the tools they need to change and transform the communities in which they reside, where the researcher operates as an
'enabler', not a 'controller'. I say this as someone who comes from a historical
background rooted in slavery and colonialism, where life has been part of a process
of self-direction and determination, as opposed to state and social dependency. It
was through engaging with my elders, ancestors, and learning about strategies for
survival from 'passed on stories. I have also observed during my years working both
in the inner city and prisons how legions of community people I have encountered
wander around aimlessly with little or no meaning to their lives or have no sense of
belonging. As a researcher it is critically important to be sensitive to the needs of
those who want to be the 'authors of their own lives'.

To be or not to be

The occupation of a different personal space to 'be' creates a newly constructed
'self' that could be articulated using performance as the conduit. Performance not
only provides the opportunity for 'self-reflection', but scope for transforming into a
new 'constructed self' while working with black offenders. In my work with black
male offenders I have used stories, creativity, and passed on wisdom to enable them
to explore and narrate their own lived realities expressed in 'dramatic form'. The
resulting outcomes at times created much-needed counter-narratives that sometimes led to small systemic changes within the regimes themselves. In some respect
working in partnership with offenders this way, using creativity as a conduit, we
actualized notions of 'praxis' (discussed later in the book). This 'counter-narrative'
construction was designed to both privilege the voices of the offenders, while at
the same time contesting some of the assumptions made by those who seldom take
into consideration the 'collective narrative' of the 'experts' and 'knowers'. It was
also a way of enabling them to transcend their silences in a way only they understand. This approach as Valdes, Culp and Harris (2002) acknowledged;

> resists the subordinating messages of the dominant culture by challenging ste-
> reotypes and presenting and representing people of colour as complex and
> heterogeneous.
>
> *(2002: 244)*

Valdes further suggests that the subordinated persons (black offenders) were able to
narrate and to interpret events in opposition to the dominant narratives (the prison
regime), alongside exposing the complexity of the issues being addressed. This

provided me with a unique creative opportunity for looking at 'race and crime' that has previously not been explored this way. McAdams (1988) advocates that individuals must gradually interrogate their 'own story' and create a space to rework it by providing their own 'counter-story'. hooks (1991) highlights that 'counter-stories' as recounted by black offenders were in a position to make sense of the racialization of the criminal justice system and its impacts on their lives. The knock-on effect was that these counter narratives played a significantly role in contesting white men's accounts of maintaining their privileged position, and in doing so be seen as posing a threat to challenging their subordinate status. hooks further suggests that when the 'radical voice speaks about domination, they are speaking to those who dominate'. hooks's assertion suggests it may be a better proposition for the oppressed and marginalized to be supported themselves in naming their own reality.

Outsider within

A further consideration comes from (Hill-Collins, 2000) who urges the 'outsider within' ways of seeing, to overcome the struggle to transcend their 'subordinate status'. This in effect means that the 'counter-narrative' acts as a catalyst for 'politicizing' the struggle as part of a wider campaign for social justice. Using culturally sensitive research methods where participants hear their own stories and the stories of others could assist in transcending black subordination, much the same way as music and dance operated throughout slavery. Hearing and making their stories told in their own words reaffirm a sense of humanity that enables them to consider different ways of constructing new ways of seeing the world. I felt, and still do, that the development of a personal counter-stories, as a wider critical narrative may offer insights oppressed peoples construct their own understandings of their oppressions. Counter narratives must therefore do the following:

1. Foreground issues of oppression and subordination.
2. Challenge the traditional research approach when explaining the experiences of oppressed and marginalized people.
3. Offer a transformative solution that will contest, challenge, and remove the
4. subordination of oppressed and marginalized people.
5. Focus on the intersectional experiences of community members in relation to their oppression and marginalisation.
6. Create a counter-narratives to highlight and contextualise community members experiences of oppression and marginalisation.

The collective counter narrative necessitates that the stories of community members operate as a way of transcending their silences, inasmuch as these stories are not often told or heard. These counter-stories must expose stories of racial privilege. They must further challenge the dominant discourse on race and racialization and demand for significant change in terms of the struggle for racial reform. To create these counter-stories data has to be found. Strauss and Corbin (1998) see 'theoretical sensitivity' as a personal quality of the researcher that indicates an awareness of the subtleties of meaning of data. One can come to the research situation with varying degrees of sensitivity depending upon previous reading and experience with, or relevant to, the data. It can also be developed further during the research process. Theoretical sensitivity refers to the attribute of having insight, the ability to give meaning to data, the capacity to understand, and ability to separate the pertinent from that which is not relevant. Counter-stories not only reiterate dominant meanings or power relations, but through retelling also contribute to the process of social change. It is also important within the development of counter-stories to examine, explore, and expose notions of colour-blindness.

Narrow confines

All of this is intended to move beyond the narrow confines of criminological research that struggles to validate, acknowledge, and indeed understand that the racialization of crime is something that cannot be ignored. By examining the colour-blind perspective more closely, this analysis teases out the differences within the colour-blind position. Colour-blindness ignores racism and bolsters white privilege. Colour-blindness hides in the unspoken landscape of human and social relations, distorting racial discourse and preventing awareness of knowledge that already exists in the real-lived experiences of community members. How then can community members envision a new narrative that moves beyond the divisions that shape their lives? It asserts that factors associated with race, racialization, and racism operate within a wide context and understands that these factors help explain racial inequality in the wider social structure. How then do community members acquire and tell their own authentic narrative when it has been shaped by a history of oppression?

Summary

This chapter laid out the foundation for 'data verbalization', calling for the need for validation of performance-driven research dissemination. It also revealed how my personal journey has assisted me in this endeavour. The importance of 'breaking free' from the neo-liberal stance within academia, by generating counter-narratives was equally an important feature within this chapter. It was equally important to recognize the role of critical theorizing in achieving this aim. This chapter concluded envisioning a way for the sub-textual aspect of research data to be heard.

Reflective questions

1. How important is taking a more critical stance when looking at the issue of research data dissemination as a whole?
2. How do you intend to develop your own counter-narrative/s with relation to aspects of your work deemed too political, risky, or non-traditional?

References

Baraka, A. (1963) *Blues People: Negro Music in White America*, New York: William Morrow & Company.
Bochner, A. (2014) *Coming to Narrative: A Personal History of Paradigm Change in the Human Sciences (Writing Lives)*, London: Routledge.
Brown, L. & Strega, S. (2005) *Research as Resistance: Critical, Indigenous, and Anti-Oppressive Approaches*, Ontario, Canada: Canadian Scholars Press/Women's Press.
Denzin, N.K. (2010) *The Qualitative Manifesto*, Walnut Creek, CA: Left Coast Press.
Denzin, N.K. & Giardana, M. (2017) *Qualitative Inquiry in Neo Liberal Times*, New York: Routledge.
Denzin, N.K. (2018) *Performance Autoethnography: Critical Pedagogy and the Politics of Culture*, London: Sage.
Du Bois, W. E. B. (1938) *The Souls of Black Folk*, New York: W.W. Norton.
Ellingson, L. (2017) *Embodiment in Qualitative Research*, London: Routledge.
Hill-Collins, P. (2000) *Black Feminist Thought*, New York: Routledge.
hooks, B. (1991) *Yearning: Race, Gender, and Cultural Politics*, Boston, MA: South End Press.
McAdams, D. (1988) *Power, Intimacy, and the Life Story*, London: Guilford Press.
Marable, M. (1995) *Beyond Black and White: Transforming African American Politics*, New York: Verso.
Mills, C.W. (1959) *The Sociological Imagination*, New York: Oxford University Press.
Ritchie, J.S. & Wilson, D.E. (2000) *Teacher Narrative as Critical Inquiry: Rewriting the Script*, New York: Teachers College Press.
Strauss, A. & Corbin, J. (1998) *Basics of Qualitative Research*, London: Sage.
Valdes, F., Culp, J., & Harris, A. (2002) *Crossroads, Directions and a New Critical Race Theory*, Philadelphia, PA: Temple Press.

2

PERFORMING RESEARCH AND PRAXIS

Conundrum

Nine men and women sit in a room; a community activist; sociologist; a criminologist; a philosopher; a scientist; an educationalist; a social worker; a church leader; and an ex-gang member. They address one question, 'How can we present a collective narrative about crime in the inner city?' After four hours of tense discussion and analysis they cannot find a unified position. Tensions flair, where there is no agreement. The meeting ends abruptly. A week later a young man is shot, several fathers go to prison, lots of women become victims of domestic violence, a range of young people are suspended from school and the community fragments and implodes on itself. The same nine individuals meet again a few weeks later to discuss what can be done. Again, there is no agreement. The group is then forced to confront a painful truth, namely, professional labels and ideological positioning doesn't always solve problems, but instead weakens the possibility of collective and transformative action.

Praxis and transformation

How do we reach a consensus about strategies designed to bring about change and transformation in the lives of oppressed and marginalized communities using research dissemination as an aid? A consideration is the way in which divisions emerge as a consequence of researchers occupying different epistemological and ontological paradigms, positions, and contexts that further divides the pathways toward achieving collective and unified research driven emancipatory goals. So, what can 'data verbalization' contribute to the understanding of '**praxis**?' Eminent Brazilian educator Paulo Freire (1970) saw education as political and must be informed by praxis. That is, challenging power relationships leading to transformative action. Carr and Kemmis (1986) state:

Praxis is a commitment to human well-being, the search for truth, and respect for others. It is the action of people who are free, who are able to act for themselves.

(1986: 190)

Actualizing 'praxis' in modern post-industrial societies could be viewed as subversive and revolutionary where ideological posturing can render the aspirations and dreams of many communities obsolete. As many of our inner cities would attest; the rise in crime, the proliferation of hostility to 'others', the threat posed by so called 'fake news', merged with a contemporary anomie (Durkheim, 1893) would suggest new solutions to old problems need to be sought. My own observations within the community I live further highlights how the rampant consumer culture that targets the poorer sections of the community leads to an onslaught of physical and existential threats manifesting in a deterioration in community life. Durkheim articulated the idea of 'anomie' around a lack of ethical or social standards where the expectations of behaviour were unclear, and the system had broken down. In essence the 'old rules no longer apply'. This would suggest that as the level of social disorganization that blights much of our inner cities, performance driven research dissemination could play a significant role in expressing ideas that could actualize 'praxis' in ways that are contemporary and relevant for today's social media laden communities. As praxis is an iterative, reflective approach to taking action, a committed researcher must be prepared to participate in 'collective ideals' in line with important community concerns. This makes contemporary approaches to actualizing 'praxis' political by default.

Transformative tools

Friere (1970) believed that oppressed peoples should see praxis as a transformative tool where the ultimate objective would be liberation from oppressive forces and ultimately transformation. Therefore, for those of us engaged in praxis-oriented research we must strive to involve the community as an integral part of the research process as a whole. As praxis has an explicit goal to empower marginalized peoples by assisting in the wider strategies for challenging oppression, the research process cannot simply be viewed as a matter of collecting and analyzing data. Praxis-oriented research should further involve establishing reciprocal working relationships between the researcher and members of the community under study. By engaging collaboratively in this way, researchers may help participants acquire the critical tools to transform their own lives. It is my view that it is in the area of dissemination (data verbalization) where the possibility for change may be seen and heard in a form that can bring clarity, focus, and direction to actions that are required to actualize 'praxis'. In essence 'data verbalization' may assist as part of a change continuum, and not be seen as an end in itself. Although our research projects may be used to gather data and build theories, social justice and transformation should be its primary goal. Friere (1970) so too recognizes that people must see the causes of their oppression, and through transforming action they can create a new situation, one which makes life better and more prosperous. This would suggest that, praxis is messy, risky, and complex, requiring a multi-pronged approach. 'Data verbalization' could open up opportunities for progressive researchers interested in situating themselves as part of revolutionary process of change to assist in changing the consciousness of the oppressed, alongside creating a 'counter-narrative' from which to form 'strategies of action'. A key consideration here is how do researchers operate and begin this journey as advocates for actualizing 'praxis' as part of research dissemination. Denzin (2018) states:

> A performance based discourse is based on minimalist principles. It shows. It doesn't tell. Less is more. It is not infatuated with theory. It uses few concepts. It is performative.
>
> *(2018: 5)*

Similar to Denzin, I argue that 'data verbalization' has an important role to play when looking at the interplay between both 'theory' and 'practice'. Adding to Denzin's perspective this chapter does not seek to present a saturated view of theoretical arguments. The functioning of this chapter is designed to engage researchers in a mature discussion that seeks to move beyond mere intellectual rhetoric, and root itself more within a grounded conversation designed to make progressive researchers consider the context laid out before them. For me it starts with the issue of positionality.

The insider and praxis

I myself operate and declare myself an 'insider researcher'. Generally, insider-researchers are those who chose to study a group to which they belong, while outsider researchers do not belong to the group under study. My insider positioning views the research process and products as co-constructions between myself and the participants in the research. I regard the research participants or respondents as active 'informants' to my research; where I attempt to give voice to the powerless in a dignified and affirming way. Although disemmination of research through speeches, PowerPoints, discussion, and more recently the 'open space' format suffices when feeding back the key messages of the research, it is questionable at times if the outcomes connect to the constituency from which the research inquiry emerged. Contained within research data are many 'subtextual messages' that can 'strenghten' and 'enhance' the overall tone of research enquries where the audience requires the information to be presented in accessible ways and easily understood. Denzin (2010) argues that for 'subordinated voices' to be heard, they must be 'helped to speak'. Equally as important is the view of Bochner (2014), who writes,

> Listening to different voices and trying to express your own, about trying to muster the courage to speak the unspoken even if it terrifies you.
>
> *(2014: 315)*

Both Denzin and Bochner highlight the need for research to reveal participants and research subject's 'own truths' and to tell their own stories if they are to transcend the limitations imposed on them. Denzin further argues for 'performative social science' paradigms that provide some new answers to old problems. In responding to issues of power and inequality Denzin calls for the construction of 'counter narratives' that will enable the 'subordinated individual or community' to both 'narrate' and 'interpret' their 'lived reality' through the 'dramatization of data'. I also contend that qualitative research methods should be transformative for both the researcher as well as for the researched. This will require moving away from obsessions with positivistic conceptions of scientific research and using other possible functions of qualitative research methods that, by nature, respect the subjective dimensions of the human experience. However, in the comfort of academia where many of us may be divorced from where the problems within society there are a range of critical questions reflexively that needs to be addressed if we are to be straight with ourselves concerning the intention behind our work. Adapted from Hamlet's soliloquy 'to be or not to be praxis that is the question'.

To be or not to be praxis?

Research dissemination, whether it is written or oral tends to take place at the end of a research project. It brings closure to processes, where a hypothesis is either proved or disproved, something amazing has emerged, awareness has been raised, or results are fed back. However, a couple of pertinent questions arise: 'Who really pays attention to the dissemination of qualitative research findings?' and more importantly 'What are the further implications and consequences of research that remains on shelves with little impact on practice, research, policy or the wider community?' To those who see the communication of qualitative research findings as part of a wider aspiration towards social justice goals/aims, it is important to have an open dialogue. As the modes of dissemination such as the journal article or conference presentation, can often alienate audiences and distance many researchers from seeing their research go from theory, practice, and finally action. It is my view that community members should be actively involved with the researcher in creating a co constructed position from which to bring 'liberatory and participatory' approaches to research dissemination to the fore. Akom (2008) argues that educators need to find numerous ways to build stronger agency within research participants by placing them in the centre of the research process, from data gathering, analysis, through to dissemination.

Whose knowledge is it?

Roy and Campbell (2015) express the view that both 'tacit' and 'explicit' knowledge should be valued within the processes used by both researcher and active informants. This knowledge should also challenge history and re-envision both theory and practice by extending and informing the original research itself. In my own discipline of criminology, Young (2011) calls for a more critical criminological imagination that moves beyond the confines of a research culture that dumbs down curiosity, instead of addressing itself directly to 'notions of power' and its wider impacts with relation to the understanding and construction of crime as a whole. Young further argues that more transformative research is required to break the barriers between the social scientist and their subjects, while at the same time facilitating change in the investigated. Not only do I echo Young's sentiments, but to actively ensure my contribution to knowledge isn't rendered 'invisible', I must both struggle and sacrifice to do so. The concept of invisibility was put forward by African American novelist Ralph Ellison (1947: 7) who wrote:

> I am an invisible man. No, I am not a spook like those who haunted Edgar Allan Poe; nor am I one of your Hollywood movie ectoplasms. I am a man of substance, of flesh and bone, fibre and liquids – and I might even be said to possess a mind. I am invisible; understand, simply because people refuse to see me.
>
> *(1947: 7)*

Ellison reminds us that being rendered invisible must be resisted at all costs and is not an option for progressive critical researchers. Our presence in the domain of research dissemination must be on-going and sustained. While validating my 'insider' positioning continues to throw up challenges, the cumulative impact of my academic 'invisibility' is made worse, when at times my insights and understandings are marginalized by those who operate from privileged epistemological and ontological vantage points within my own institution. Brown and Strega (2005) issue a challenge to all researchers by asking us to engage in research practices from a position of solidarity with the marginalised.

Knock knock, who's there?

Again, some researchers I have encountered are what Du Bois (1978) refers to 'carwash sociologists' who do not venture into communities, and as Katz (1988) reminds us many other social scientists can graciously transport themselves to worlds they have never been but make claims from the safe vantage point of the so-called 'ivory tower'. How then do we then (re)present the experiences of marginalized populations in ways that are accessible, informative, and transformative? It would be easy to formulate solutions that are out of sync with the reality of their lives. However, if we do not find new ways of presenting the complexities faced by the disaffected sections of communities, then it could be argued that research feeds a deterministic narrative. The world is at times messy, dangerous, and chaotic and cannot always been measured objectively or be quantified by assumptions that omit the awkwardness, helplessness, and disaffection that at times does not make its way into the final research report. hooks (1991) so too reminds us that when marginalized voices speak to power, they are speaking to those who dominate. It is my view that it may be a better proposition for researchers such as myself to assist and support communities in 'naming their own reality' by using research dissemination politically, and to further consider how we can institutionalize those ways of seeing that will enable some of us to transcend our subordinate status within the academy as a whole.

Risk factor

It is indeed my experience that for researchers like myself who undertake so called 'risky research', we can be excluded from major research bids, never taken seriously by other academics, and pushed out forums who feel that objectivity, longitudinal studies, and abstract concepts, takes precedence over research that speaks to power. Thus, the transformative power of research may have more currency if expressed creatively, connected to networks that become gateways for change and transformation. The essential characteristics of transformational research could best be described as being subjective, relational, collaborative, interpretive, and performative. Mills (1959) sees that individuals can better understand their experiences by becoming aware of those of all individuals in similar circumstances. Mills further sees the importance of rooting the 'sociological imagination' within a context that enables us to grasp both history and biography within society, and to explore the relationship between the two. Brown and Strega (2005) also express the view that there must be a willingness to explore the emancipatory possibilities of new approaches to research, even when these transgress the boundaries of traditional research and scholarship. It is my view that knowledge production should be assessed based on legitimizing excluded information generated by progressive researchers in ways that are rooted in ways of 'knowing' that are not defined by 'privileged others'. If knowledge creation and expression is separated from actualizing 'praxis' how do we then grasp the messy complexities of people's lives, especially the lives of those on the margins. For me it must involve reclaiming hidden and lost knowledge whilst at the same time creating new 'counter-narratives' that move us away from binary conceptualizations that are fostered under existing oppressive research paradigms.

Othering

Indeed, my observations in connection to and engagement with, the criminal justice system over the last three decades would suggest that the current so-called mainstream framing of much research with relation to community development and social transformation is deeply flawed, inward looking, and does little for responding to the shifting patters of inequality within a global context. It is my assertion that unless we comprehend how notions of the 'other' are constructed and acted upon, we will merely continue to reproduce and reinforce a continuing legacy of privileged dominance. Equally as important is to reconcile the contextual understandings and differences that underpin the binary of the 'global north–south divide'. Again, I would like to turn my attention to my own discipline of criminology where the hegemonic assumptions that underpins so much 'theorizing crime'. I am calling for the development of a 'counter narrative' as a way of both revising the discipline, alongside using a praxis-oriented strategy to bring change to the discipline as a whole. It is evident that the lack of unification, awareness, or connections between global north–south criminological theorists, writers, academics, etc. is something that must be bridged if we are to have a truly inclusive and more rounded representation of criminology in the future. In essence it is envisioned that by bringing the global north–south divide together, we will be able to engage in a dialogue based less on separation, privilege, and cultural dominance, and more on mutual respect for other perspectives that are not being seen, heard, or acknowledged within the current global north dominance within so-called contemporary 'mainstream criminology'.

Counter narratives

Presenting a 'counter narrative' to the dominant 'majoritarian narrative' that current exists will not only challenge the myth of criminological meritocracy but expose criminological privilege in the process. By placing 'race and the racialization of crime' at the centre of their analysis and moving away from paradigms that hold whiteness within criminology as the norm, critical race scholarship in criminology must identify research agendas that incorporate collective actions taken by an inclusive cohort of 'activists scholars' committed to the struggle for academic validation. This position would suggest that the criminological project is both incomplete and lacking unless there is a wider validation and inclusion of the contribution of excluded and marginalized non-white and progressive white scholars when looking at the racialization of crime, as well as crime as a whole. A need for a criminological counter narrative is now required. Critical Race Theory (CRT) can also be used as a discourse for liberation, as well as methodological and epistemological tools to expose the ways 'race and racism' affect the lives of racialized minorities within global criminal justice systems. Delgado and Stefancic (2005) cite several tenets that locate CRT as an analytical framework:

- Racism is ordinary, not exceptional, and it is the usual way that society does business. Its ordinariness makes racism hard to recognize and much less easy to address.
- The social construction of race, and the related idea of differential racialization, hold that race and races are products of social thought.
- Not objective, inherent, or fixed, races correspond to no simple biological or genetic reality; rather, they are categories that society invents for particular purposes, usually ignoble ones.
- Building on this insight, differential racialization calls attention to the ways in which the dominant society racializes different minority groups in different ways at different times in response to shifting needs.

Valdes, Culp and Harris (2002) too acknowledges that CRT 'resists the subordinating messages of the dominant culture by challenging stereotypes and presenting and representing people of colour as complex and heterogeneous' (2002:

244). Valdes further suggests that CRT not only can enable the subordinated persons to narrate, to interpret events in opposition to the dominant narratives (of white men), but also recognizes the complexity of the issues being addressed. The narrative potential of CRT therefore lies in 'its ability to re-story the past and to then re-imagine the future'. CRT offers new insights with which to explore and explain the understanding processes of the racialization of crime/criminal justice systems and its impacts on the desistance process, for black men. CRT's use of storytelling as its analytical framing provided a unique creative opportunity to look at the role of narrative in desistance, a position previously not explored in this context. CRT operates with two distinct storytelling paradigms. 'Majoritarian stories' told by privileged white people, and 'counter-stories' told by subordinated black people (Solorzano & Yosso, 2002).

Our stories

McAdams advocates the interrogation of one's own story and creating a space to rework it by the development of a 'counter-story'. hooks (1991) highlights that black men's 'counter-stories', when they do contest white men's accounts of maintaining their privileged position, are seen as posing a threat by challenging their subordinate status. hooks further argues that when radical voices speak, they are speaking to directly to those who dominate. hooks's assertion suggests it may be a better proposition to further consider how progressive researchers can encourage and institutionalize 'outsider within' ways of seeing, to overcome the struggle of having an academic 'subordinate status' (Hill-Collins, 2000: 29). Bell (1992) also calls for a 'racial realism' that advocates for racial reform, with a focus that responds to recurring aspects of the subordinate status that impedes the development of marginalized groups such as black offenders within society. The need for transcendent change is at the core of Bell's thinking. Differential racialization calls attention to the way the dominant society racializes different groups, in different ways, in different times, with relation to structures such as the criminal justice system. Therefore, differential racialization applied to criminology needs to look at, and address, how the discipline structures and constructs its insights and understandings of 'race and racialization' with relation to crime as a whole. The ability to contest this position of 'differential racialization' involves interrogating how the narrative of so-called mainstream contemporary criminology is produced, produces, or does not produce change. It may require progressive researchers who believe in the value of diversification in criminology, to seek new, improved, and contemporary solutions in way crime are constructed, researched, analysed, and acted upon. How then does the discipline of so-called mainstream criminology engage in a critical dialogue that will ensure that theoretical criminological perspectives from progressive criminology scholars moves the discourse beyond mere privileged gestures coming from so called mainstream criminology? Cuneen and Rowe (2014) argue that there have been limited attempts to consider the theoretical and practice implications of indigenous understandings and approaches to the discipline of criminology. They further argue that criminology is equally as slow in recognizing the importance of understanding the way in which colonial effects are perpetuated through knowledge control, particularly in relation to criminal justice systems. Carrington, Hog and Sozzo (2016) similarly argue that criminology's of the global south have by and large accepted their subordinate role within the global organization of knowledge to the detriment of occupying a prominent role within the wider global discipline of criminology itself. Both Carrington et al. and Cuneen and Rowe's assertions provides an important entry point for positioning 'intersectionality' as a key theoretical framework when considering praxis.

Intersectionality

Relying too heavily on concepts of race, class, and gender operating as independent variables, without acknowledging that society has now firmly moved into a digital, virtual, and on-line mediated space, can be problematic. A suggested framework such as intersectionality may provide a possible solution. Intersectionality as Crenshaw (1999) argues is the understanding that human beings are shaped by the interaction of their different social locations which occur within a context of connected systems and structures of power. Crenshaw sees such processes as being where independent and multiple forms of privilege and oppression are created. Crenshaw further argues that intersectionality understands that human beings are shaped by the interaction of different social locations, connected systems, and structures of power. Hill-Collins & Bilge (2016) highlight how intersectionality if not properly understood risks missing the process of discovery that underlies how people actually use intersectional frameworks. Hill-Collins & Bilge further see intersectionality as a form of critical praxis referring in ways in which groups draw upon or use intersectional frameworks in their daily lives for transformative purposes. Critical praxis therefore constitutes an important feature of intersectional inquiry that is both attentive to intersecting power relations, alongside providing the impetus for resisting the imposition of social inequality. Hill-Collins & Bilge also argue that not all critical thinking is confined to the academy, nor is political engagement found solely in social movements and see it as shorthand for the link between critical inquiry and practice. A praxis-oriented approach to research dissemination therefore does not merely apply scholarly knowledge to a social problem or set of experiences but rather uses knowledge learned within everyday life to reflect on those every day experiences informed by scholarly knowledge. This scholarly approach does not separate itself out from practice, or from the people who have to apply the emerging outcomes ideas in real life settings connected, to real life problems. The work of Brazilian theatre director Augusto Boal is relevant here.

Data verbalization – Re-storying oppression

Boal (1993) encouraged critical thought about social conditions using theatre as the conduit and developed the 'Theatre of the Oppressed' to great artistic and intellectual acclaim. Boal was in sympathy with the oppressed and believed in 'theatre as praxis'. Over the years much of my own work in criminal justice, public health, and education has built on his creative and philosophical ideas, which has in turn informed the direction of my future work. Similar to Boal, I believe that those of us who are engaged in 'critical enquiry' should utilize 'performative approaches' when conducting research that is socially and culturally driven. This approach serves as a tool for both maximizing the potential of research that affects people's lives, alongside increasing the potential 'impact' of the research itself with relation to personal, community, and social transformation/change. Working as a researcher I have observed how both 'quantitative' and 'qualitative' research reports can at times be disseminated through traditional means; conferences, seminars, workshops, etc. where the format is predictable and important messages can get 'lost in translation'. This in my view weakens the research as a whole if the 'feedback-sharing' of the outcomes are relegated to mere 'sound bites' or 'small chunks of information' that may raise awareness but doesn't provide the impetus that will see the implementation of key recommendations brought to fruition. This state of affairs is at best troubling especially when the demand of much contemporary research is to:

- Make a difference.
- Give value for money.
- Be groundbreaking in its visioning, scope, and impact.

'Performance driven research dissemination' such as data verbalization may offer important opportunities when presenting research that can be experienced through active 'observation', 'participation', and 'interaction'. In doing so the representations of data provide a unified benefit for all of those involved in the process as a whole, funders included. As a dramatist I have been fortunate enough to have had many of my ideas produced for the stage, screen, and radio. Similarly, my academic work has been enhanced by using 'creative approaches' when conducting my research, whether it using creativebeit 'methods', or in the 'dissemination process'. The need to 'perform research' therefore is a 'call to arms' for all of those who want to ensure that the work we do is connected to the widest constituency of 'influence' and 'impact'. Before, during, and after my doctoral studies I encountered many of my colleagues who were, and are, looking for a creative outlet for their own research as they want to reach a bigger audience, and to generate impact beyond the confines of the academy, report, or dissertation/thesis. I therefore vowed to create something for those silent voices contained within my research to be seen and heard, as well as enabling other researchers to develop their own bespoke ways of promoting and presenting their research presented in forms that are transformative, participatory, and creative in orientation. For progressive researchers wanting to embrace an adapted 'Frierian' approach to disseminating their research using 'performance driven' approaches, I needed to focus on some of the key pointers of the researcher operating from a standpoint of a 'participatory educator'.

Researcher as participatory educator

I define a 'participatory educator' as:

> A 'visionary' individual who is recognized for their insights, expertize, and wisdom. They are actively sought out, engaged with, provide formal/informal support and guidance, as well as acting in the capacity of both a 'mediator' and 'advocate' around a diverse range of issues.
>
> *(Glynn, 2016)*

Denzin et al. (2003) argues that qualitative research exists in a time of global uncertainty and expresses further expresses the view that governments are attempting to regulate scientific inquiry by defining what constitutes 'good' science. Denzin is strident in his view where he urges progressive researchers to be cognizant of regulatory activities that threatens critical and radical scholarship in the academy. Hare (1973) asked black scholars and sociologists to question their positionality with relation to academia and suggested that it wasn't a simple case of turning up at university and just reading and writing. Hare further asked black scholars to move beyond mere 'academic idealism' by 'decolonizing the mind' as a part of a process that laid the groundwork for others to follow. In essence, Hare wanted black scholars to seek liberation from oppressive forces by becoming 'participatory educators'. Of late I have noticed how the debates between some scholars still focuses on issues of tenure, with little scope for engaging in a dialogue about how we locate our intellectual pursuits within a wider context of social justice and more importantly, liberation for the hearts and minds of the wider community. For me it is appropriate to revisit Hare's assertions, but this time adapting them in relation to the key responsibilities of the researcher as 'participatory educator'. Those of us who operate from a privileged vantage point have both a duty of care and an ethical responsibility to support the marginalized and disaffected sections of the community in finding creative spaces and platforms at a time where effective and motivational leadership is conspicuously absent. I have identified ten key guiding principles for the 'participatory educator' to consider:

1. The 'participatory educator' must recognize and study historical movements and ancient forms of transformative pedagogy, combined with investigating the nature of pedagogy itself. An example would be how slaves organized and educated themselves during a time when learning was banned or forbidden on the plantation. Many oppressed and marginalized communities have been stripped of both their history and culture where teachings, insights, and understandings have remained hidden. There is much to learn and gain from past historical insights in terms of learning. By revising the past, we may be able to bring some important meanings into new contexts and situations.
2. The 'participatory educator' must not suffer from the problem of economic dependency and the increasing monopoly of the world of funding, publications,

and dissemination of their ideas/philosophy. Education should not be confined or constrained purely by a lack of economic resources. Having worked in prisons for many years, I have witnessed many purposeful and innovative approaches to engaging offenders, that are not rooted in large budget, but more of bringing participatory learning styles and approaches to the fore.

3. The 'participatory educator' must transcend Western concepts of pedagogy and embrace indigenous, non-traditional, and culturally competent forms of pedagogy. Those of us who live in privileged northern hemispheric environments should actively seek out and engage southern hemispheric approaches to pedagogy; indigenous epistemologies that include spirituality; marginalized pedagogies such as those proffered by offenders, offer a range of innovative approaches to learning connected to rehabilitative processes; and intergenerational pedagogies which uses more culturally competent generative learning styles and approaches, creates significant scope for the participatory educator who desires to broaden their epistemological horizons.

4. The 'participatory educator' must look below the surface of things and, wherever necessary and appropriate, take a stand against epistemologies and pedagogies that oppresses community members desire to learn and transform their lives. This position in essence moves the participatory educator from a passive to active role, firmly rooted in the pursuit of social justice and community transformation. Much of my own learning has been taken up with contesting and challenging biased assumptions, beliefs, and values that has erased much of my own social, political, and historical past. In essence I have at times had to go in search of hidden truths, alongside conducting my research.

5. The 'participatory educator' must reject the notion that it is not professional to be emotional, opinionated, and to operate through neutrality. If you are privileged, there is no need to seek redress or struggle with claims of validity and reliability. However, as a non-white scholar I have not had the luxury of operating through neutrality. In saying that the processes I use, engage with, and promote, are subject to the same scrutiny in terms of ethics, values, and judgements. Within my own positionality I too will have subjective bias, opinions, alongside emotional conflicts along the journey of my research. Therefore, in recognizing my own positioning, I am also accepting that in the struggle for social justice I cannot see myself operating neutrally. As a researcher I am a contributor to the struggle, not the whole struggle itself.

6. The 'participatory educator' must develop new and appropriate norms, values, methods, modes of analysis, operations, etc. in order to be effective. Again, I must return to a previous point. There are many contemporary influences on our work; social media, TV, globalization, etc. This must make us cognizant at all times regarding how we engage with society. By operating as a bricoleur I have embraced and indeed used other mediums to inform my research dissemination strategy, as a way of contributing not just to ideas within society, but to how recipients of my ideas can use them to actualize some of their own needs and concerns. Similarly, I have been fortunate enough to have

engaged with scholars from other cultures and research traditions that has enabled me to broaden my epistemological horizons.

7. The 'participatory educator' must understand the social function of scholarship and must re-assess the traditions, values and context of Western scholarship. Having taught on a black studies degree, alongside conduct critical race research, I have concluded that the workings of society cannot be purely engaged with, if they contribute to, and further my oppression. It is also my experience of insights coming from indigenous and incarcerated scholars has pushed me to consider how my own work can be enhanced by studying those who have succeeded in bringing scholarship, pedagogy, and social change to the vanguard of change overall. The works of educator Paulo Friere and theatre maker Augusto Boal are exemplary examples.

8. The 'participatory educator' main task is to shape the collective consciousness with ideas, thoughts, and a vision that is both motivating and inspiring. With the pilot phase of data verbalization, it was clearly evident how much community people engaged with the simplification of complex ideas through performance. Although not fully representative, the feedback on mediums such as LinkedIn, Twitter, Facebook, radio programmes, etc., would suggest that the emotional impact in areas such as motivation and inspiration are important considerations when embarking on the journey of participatory and emancipatory education through research dissemination.

9. The 'participatory educator' must pursue of new ways of 'seeing' and 'being' through bringing together of contemporary knowledge and ancient wisdom. A friend once told me that the elders are our textbooks. The relevance here is to always strive for locating some of what we do within an intergenerational context. Knowledge does not always emerge from government-funded projects, peer review sanctions, or exclusive academic institutions. We should constantly be striving to detect, uncover, and expose ourselves to ontological ways of experiencing the world. Within the realms of culture and spirituality there are insights, experiences, and ways of knowing that offer much possibilities. In order to embrace these possibilities, we must be open at all times to experiencing things that will put us out of our comfort zone.

10. The 'participatory educator' must remain vigilant at all times, recognizing the need to change as and when required. A committed 'participatory educator' must be someone who acknowledges that liberation from oppressive forces must be a key goal when leading communities who themselves require support in transforming their pain and suffering into healing and transformation.

It is my contention that residents of inner-city communities where I reside and work, are exposed to many social determinants of health. It is to this end that I see them as both the 'experts' and 'knowers' of their own experiences, in spite of the barriers they face. In a world of binaries inner-city communities are often portrayed as 'no go' zones, places to pass through, and not to live. Seldom is the resilience, cohesion, and strength of those who live under difficult circumstances acknowledged in an academic world that would rather create a nightmare scenario, than one of occupying a difficult space and thriving. The inner-city communities I'm referring to, and am connected with give the world so many positive things that are seldom, explored in crime dramas, reality TV shows, or indeed academic journals. Much about what I've read about my reality paints a picture that not only distorts it but generates subtle forms of 'moral panic' that creates a world that is portrayed as hedonistic, lawless, and 'crime ridden'. The inner-city communities I visit and live amongst offer researchers multiple opportunities to engage in a dialogue around those same understandings, thoughts, feelings, insights, and experiences through telling their own stories and more importantly in their own words. Researchers operating as participatory educators must therefore speak to those excluded, marginalized, and neglected individuals and communities, who like me, feel it is time for our voices to be heard, as well as exercising our right to contest the views of those who 'talk cricket from the boundary, but seldom face a fast bowler from the crease'. The 'ebony tower' is relevant here as it is an 'inclusive' not 'exclusive' space. It starts from a position that acknowledges the limitations of any researcher can be strengthened by a community's engagement and involvement with the formulation, undertaking, and dissemination of ideas related to those things that will have impact on their lives. How then do progressive researchers maintain the balance between challenging the status quo, while at the same time not being sucked in to the very machinery that grinds their energy down? The following case example is an illustration of what is possible with relation to 'data verbalization' playing a role in actualising something that would loosely be seen as 'praxis-oriented'.

Case example: Gangs and desistance

A close friend and colleague, involved in 'outreach work' with young people at risk of serious youth violence was complaining that young people he worked with were 'switching off' from listening to messages given to them by adults and older people in general. In his conversations he remarked how hip-hop, grime, and social media were much more powerful medium that influenced the young people we worked with. Frustrated by this state of affairs he began to question his ability as a youth worker to continually engage young people as he couldn't compete with the negative influences coming from the streets via the music and social media. On sending him a copy of my first data verbalization single 'Silenced', he began to engage young people in a musical form they related to, with messages that reflected their reality. The young people started to listen and process what they were listening to. When my friend revealed what they were listening to, something transformative happened. They wanted to meet me for further discussions about their concerns. Located in a community setting many of these young people attended what could best described as a 'community forum'. These young people all came from difficult backgrounds and were deemed unreachable. In our prevailing discussions it transpired that many of them desired to reconnect to education, terminate their negative behaviour, and contribute to the development of the next generation. The outcome was that my friend had found a new and informed what to communicate with his young people, alongside enhancing his own practice. He now uses 'data verbalization' as part of his group work practice, alongside some of his young people who are now using the method to enhance their own performance skills and abilities.

Conclusion

This chapter called for the acknowledgement that some aspects of research encounters are not uniform; do not take place in safe environments, and at times struggle with notions of objectivity. It further sees that for progressive researchers working 'outside the box' must struggle against accepting notions of irrelevant and inappropriate methods of research dissemination. This chapter further calls for progressive researchers to be both vigilant and defiant in the face of continuing and sustainable pressure coming from forces designed to keep controversial and challenging out of the public gaze. If progressive researchers are rendered powerless in an academic system that privileges one group over the other, then access to our research and the methods we employ will also be rendered obsolete. For those researchers who suffer disparities in their work to successfully operate independently of street level bureaucrats, policy makers, and strategic agencies is problematic and requires a new approach that provides a shared platform that has power to determine its own destiny. Without a clear, precise, and focussed approach to challenging power within our society, we will merely replicate the same oppressive structures we are desiring to change. Therefore if progressive researchers are to transcend their subordination, then they must seek transformative spaces where the interrogation of the obstacles and barriers to their 'freedom of academic speech' is given voice, complete with the development of an action plan designed to push their counter narrative into a strategy for meaningful and productive change. The current state of affairs leaves little room for intellectual growth, when these very definitions create a powerless and subordinate group who languish in the research abyss hoping something will turn up. Future research dissemination strategies must both challenge dominant social and cultural assumptions regarding the researcher's ability to name their own reality, alongside using the outcomes of their research to actualise 'praxis'. In doing so any future research must develop counter discourses through storytelling, narratives, chronicles, and biographies that draw on our lived experiences of the silent, invisible, and marginalized. Until such time performed 'counter narratives' using methods such as 'data verbalization' may give progressive researchers a viable platform to bring important ideas to wider audiences seeking change and transformation. As many researchers are situated differently in relation to the economic, political, and social worlds of academic research and funding, searching for new sources of support, forging stronger and more effective unions with other outside the academy becomes a prerequisite. As I ponder my own future in academia I have come to a deeper realisation. The existential question before me is less about embracing my academic identity and more about focussing on 'what kind of academic do I want to continue to be?' The future may be uncertain and full of trepidation, but I have given myself permission to pursue my intellectual freedom. A few words to those who want to join me or to those who want to stop me. I would like to offer a few lines of a poem I found tucked away in my reflexive diary;

I will no longer be bound by notions of race
I will no longer be held captive or lost without trace
I will no longer be trapped by bein' told I'm not equal
I will no longer be concerned with reruns or sequels
My freedom ain't a mystery, nor wrapped up in clues
Or based on your theories, or relies on your views
It emerges from struggle, commitment, and toil
Shaped by my needs, with a passion that's loyal
My freedom is here, right now.
And I'm taking it
As I will no longer defend my right to be me
Who will run alongside me?

Summary

This chapter started by posing some questions regarding the complexities of research decision making as a precursor to exploring the role of 'praxis' within the dissemination process. By exploring praxis with relation to; the insider researcher, counter narratives as praxis, and praxis and intersectionality, the intention was to provoke further discussion in an underdeveloped area of epistemological concerns that requires all researchers to be more cognizant of. The chapter concluded with an exploration of the 'Researcher as a participatory educator'. Important here was the need to look at a contentious issue of impact beyond the academy.

Key questions

1. How important is the researcher's role as a 'participatory educator'?
2. What are the consequences of taking up such a position?
3. How important is actualising 'praxis' is your own research work?

References

Akom, A. (2008) 'Black metropolis and mental life: Beyond the burden of "acting white": Toward a third wave of Critical Racial Studies', *Anthropology and Education Quarterly*, 39(3): 247–265.

Bell, D. (1996) *Gospel Choirs*, New York: Basic Books.

Bell, D. (2003) 'Telling tales: What stories can teach us about racism', *Race, Ethnicity and Education*, 6(1): 3–28.

Boal, A. (1993) *Games for Actors and Non-Actors*, London: Routledge.

Bochner, A. (2014) *Coming to Narrative: A Personal History of Paradigm Change in the Human Sciences (Writing Lives)*, London: Routledge.

Brown, L. & Strega, S. (2005) *Research as Resistance: Critical, Indigenous, and Anti-Oppressive Approaches*, Ontario, Canada: Canadian Scholars Press/Women's Press.

Carrington, K., Hog, R., & Sozzo, M. (2016) 'Southern Criminology', *The British Journal of Criminology*, 56(1): 1–20.

Carr, W. & Kemmis, S. (1986) *Becoming Critical: Education, Knowledge and Action Research*, London: Falmer.

Crenshaw, K. (1999) 'Mapping the margins: Intersectionality, identity politics and violence against women of color', *Stanford Law Review*, 43: 1241–1299.

Cunneen, C. & Rowe, S. (2014) 'Changing narratives: Colonised peoples, criminology and social work', *International Journal for Crime, Justice, and Social Democracy*, 3(1): 49–67.

Delgado, R. & Stefancic, J. (2005) *The Role of Critical Race Theory in Understanding Race, Crime, and Justice Issues*, New York: John Jay College.

Denzin, N.K. (2003) 'Reading and writing performance', *Qualitative Research*, 3(2): 243–268.

Denzin, N.K. (2010) *The Qualitative Manifesto*, Walnut Creek, CA: Left Coast Press.

Denzin, N.K. (2018) *Performance Autoethnography: Critical Pedagogy and the Politics of Culture*, London: Sage.

Du Bois, W.E.B. (1938) *The Souls of Black Folk*, New York: W.W. Norton.

Du Bois, W.E.B. (1978) *On Sociology and the Black Community*, Chicago, IL: University of Chicago Press.

Durkheim, E. (1893) *The Division of Labour in Society*, New York: Free Press.

Ellison, R. (1947) *Invisible Man*, London: Penguin.

Freire, P. (1970) *Pedagogy of the Oppressed*, London: Continuum.

Glynn, M. (2016) 'Platform "Data Verbalization Lab" Creative Dissemination of Research Data', *Stage (Project Report)*, Birmingham, UK: Birmingham City University.

Hare, N. (1973) The Challenge of a Black Scholar, In: J. Ladner, *The Death of White Sociology*, pp. 67–78, Baltimore, MD: Black Classic Press.

Hill-Collins, P. (2000) *Black Feminist Thought*, New York: Routledge.

Hill Collins, P., & Bilge, S. (2016). *Intersectionality*, Malden, MA: Polity Press.

hooks, B. (1991) *Yearning: Race, Gender, and Cultural Politics*, Boston, MA: South End Press.

Katz, J. (1988) *Seductions of Crime: Moral and Sensual Attraction of Doing Evil*, New York: Perseus Books.

Mills, C.W. (1959) *The Sociological Imagination*, New York: Oxford University Press.

Roy, S. & Campbell, B. (2015) 'An indigenous epistemological approach to promote health through effective knowledge translation', *Journal of Indigenous Research*, 4: 1–8.

Solorzano, D. & Yosso, T. (2002) 'Critical race methodology: Counterstorytelling as an analytical framework', *Qualitative Inquiry*, 8(1): 23–44.

Valdes, F., Culp, J., & Harris, A. (2002) *Crossroads, Directions and a New Critical Race Theory*, Philadelphia, PA: Temple Press.

Williams, P. (1997) *Seeing a Colour Blind Future – The paradox of race*, London: Virago.

Young, J. (2011) *The Criminological Imagination*, Cambridge, MA: Polity Press.

3

DATA VERBALIZATION AND BRICOLAGE

This chapter urges progressive researchers to employ performance-driven research dissemination strategies and approaches such as 'data verbalization' rooted within the 'bricolage' tradition. The French word 'bricoleur' describes an individual who makes use of the tools available to complete a task. Put simply, the idea that research dissemination can rely solely on the peer review journal, conferences, or small 'talk shop' gatherings to generate 'reach' and 'impact' is no longer a realistic proposition. For research to have sufficient 'data capital' there are a range of emerging concerns and considerations that now require a plethora of approaches to accommodate the complexities of contemporary expectations of research as a whole. With the proliferation of social media platforms strategies for research dissemination must consider how these new challenges associated with locating research in the wider public domain can be operationalized. Researchers based in universities should not see themselves as the sole agent for the presentation of research to either their peers or the wider community. An additional consideration is how progressive researchers can acquire the necessary tools to keep up with the rapid changes taking place brought about by these new platforms.

Committed to change

Employing the use of 'bricolage' approaches to research dissemination such as 'data verbalization' requires a movement of committed scholar-activists, practitioners, and other related individuals to create, develop, and express ways of presenting their epistemological concerns using creative means. Within the discipline of cultural criminology for example Ferrell, Hayward, and Young (2008) call for oppositional scholarship that actively seeks to dissolve conventional understandings and accepted boundaries within research. Similarly, I believe there is a need to reinvigorate a critical discussion about how the convergence of multiple perspectives and approaches to (performance-driven) research dissemination are given voice. In a world blighted by numerous problems and conflicts, research dissemination must advocate for solutions for oppressed and marginalized peoples, and not merely posit explanations that provide cute institution sound bites, combined with promoting academic egos. This chapter further invites researchers to disrupt constraining research paradigms.

Positionality

As stated previously I have had a career spanning over three decades working mainly within the criminal justice system. In that time much of the research I have conducted has been marginalized as I have refused to accept the imposition of a privileged research paradigms that have forced me at times to compromise or moderate notions of my racialized identity. This has led to my work being ignored by many academics. However, based on me taking a stand for my scholarship my research constituencies have embraced my work fully. By choosing not to respond to the comfort of scholar elitism that is so prevalent into today's neo-liberal 'target' driven academic market place, I have also paid the price in terms of academic validation; such as promotion, distribution of my work, and lack of interest from academics who run scared of 'race' and 'intersectional' approaches to research. I'm old school as I firmly believe that my research dissemination should be open, transparent, inclusive, and impacting, not pandering to the narcissism of any institution that wants more compliance over the promotion of ideas that sit outside the academy. Rogers (2012) argues that scholars and researchers who adopt bricolage do so with a recognition that the approach pushes the borders of traditional multi-methods qualitative research. Bricolage therefore should address the complex political, social, and cultural nature of conducting research itself and not adhere rigidly to scientific methods. Performance-driven research methods such as data verbalization should enable the researcher to immerse themselves fully in the practice of making artistic choices from academic data. This view may put fear into some researchers who somehow feel they can remove themselves from the connectivity to the world in which they are engaging with. Again, the binary of objectivity versus subjectivity raises its ugly head.

Solving the dilemma

Using the bricolage approach would solve such a dilemma as it recognizes that a unification of both the subjective and objective may be a better option. Surely, isn't that the basis of the mixed-methods approach that recognizes that no one method can address the whole issues under investigation. Surely, can't the same be said for research dissemination? Phillimore, Humphries, Klaas, and Knecht (2016) sees some 'bricoleurs' as being motivated by social needs where they can leverage their expertise to support the building of much-needed 'social capital' in communities blighted by difficult circumstances. Phillimore et al. further argue that social bricoleurs can also identify local opportunities and deliver services to the disadvantaged in a way that others cannot as they have inter-connected knowledge of local conditions and the resources required to affect change. The solutions they can develop may be small in scale and limited in scope, but they can assist in helping solve local social problems. Bricolage employed socially can therefore respond quickly to changing circumstances in ways that traditional forms of applying our research outcomes will struggle. However, reliance on resources and improvisation rather than formal planning sometimes prevents larger needs from being addresses. This would suggest that the success to social bricolage is in the identification and targeting of the appropriate need with the relevant methods, which should underpin any research endeavour. Critics will argue that pushing concepts such as 'the bricolage' means that progressive researchers must maintain theoretical coherence and epistemological innovation at all times. It is to the complexities and contradictions of researching 'race and racialization within criminology' I want to turn to, as a way of illustrating the need for the bricolage in performance driven research dissemination as a tool for marginalized researchers such as myself that is subjective, political, and unapologetic for its stance. Like a witness for the defence I would like to call upon on one of the earliest and most significant 'social bricoleurs', W.E.B. Du Bois.

W.E.B. Du Bois – Sociological Bricoleur

W.E.B. Du Bois (1868–1963) was significant in the struggle for racial reform in the United States. Du Bois's classic study 'The Philadelphia Negro', published in 1899, was a ground breaking sociological study of the city's African American community. As a social scientist, Du Bois used urban ethnography, social history, and descriptive statistics to challenge racism and advocated for institutional change. In essence, Du Bois employed an approach that would loosely be defined as 'bricolage'. Although Du Bois researched 'race and crime' back at beginning of the twentieth century most of those who gained prominence in terms of researching the issues were White, whereas Du Bois was African American. Du Bois raised important questions about conceptual and methodological tools for analyzing the changing and evolving patterns of 'race' in contemporary societies, with specific reference to crime. Du Bois positioned his arguments with a prophetic gaze with relation to concerns centring on 'race' should focus on social environments. Denzin (2010) expresses the view that critical qualitative scholars must transcend the limitations and constraints of politically conservative post-positivism if postmodern democracy is to succeed. What seems evident however, is that many research agendas are still overtly textual and theory-driven. If anything, there is a hastening retreat from research methods styles of research that are creative led in orientation.

No neutrality

Lather (1986) argues that once we recognize that just as there is no neutral education there is no neutral research, we no longer need apologize for unabashedly ideological research and its open commitment to using research to criticize and change the status quo. Research that involves participants in the planning, execution, and dissemination of social research could be deemed 'bricolage' with relation to power sharing. It could also be argued that researchers confronting issues of empirical accountability in their methodological choices need to search for workable ways of gathering and disseminating data creatively. Articulating notions of bricolage within methodology could be an important consideration for progressive researchers to consider. Lather (1986) calls for critical inquiry as a response to the experiences, desires, and needs of oppressed people. Du Bois's importance therefore is not just rooted in his epistemological concerns, but the importance of keeping a historical continuum as part of an on-going dialogue regarding the employment of numerous strategies (bricolage) in the pursuit of wider social and racial justice goals. For critical and progressive researchers then, moving beyond the restrictions placed on our research efforts requires new techniques and concepts for disseminating research which avoids the pitfalls of the imposition of what constitutes notions of 'reliability' and 'validity'. Furthermore, we must resist those forces who feel that only privileged and elitist forms of distribution of ideas associated with our research should form the benchmark of who is 'in' or 'out'. How then does the researcher employing the use of 'bricolage' become an advocate for change, while at the same time remain true to their research identity? Employing bricolage approaches to performance-driven research dissemination advocates for an increased democratization of disseminating research as a whole. It is to my own work within criminology I turn again. Race and racism have become huge areas of study in the social sciences over the past two decades. However, while this has been reflected in the growing body of theoretical- and empirically-based work, surprisingly little has been published exploring the methodological and practical issues involved in researching 'race and crime' creatively. Even less so where dissemination is concerned. I have no empirical data to know where all the research that has been published has been deposited, who is influenced by it, or where it is located. Obviously, when undertaking literature reviews, I can identify the breadth of ideas associated with race and the criminal justice system. What is less apparent is, who outside of the academy is the beneficiary of careful and considered research? I myself discovered the works of most black scholars not through peer review journals, but through uncovering the 'hidden history' that tried to conceal it from those of us who would eventually use it in the fight for social and racial justice. While the struggle for validating the minority scholarly contribution to criminology continues to throw up challenges, the generation, maintenance, and sustainability of this academic 'subordination' must be contested. It is for this reason that I now want to turn my attention to 'Bricolage and the researcher's imagination'.

Bricolage and the researcher's imagination

In my work as a researcher I have similarly observed how much research is disseminated where the format at times is traditional, predictable, and at worst tired. It is for this reason that I wanted to generate wider impact for research data that languishes on shelves, seldom moving beyond the confines of the academy. The struggle we have at times to expose the oppressive nature of those structures that covertly shape our research narratives, can be best addressed by employing a bricolage approach. Such an approach has at times demanded a new level of research 'self-consciousness' with relation to the numerous contexts in which I operate. As I have endeavoured to reveal my connection to those same oppressive structures the bricolage makes my way/s of seeing, hearing, and doing research, a concrete reality. In doing so I have had to come to terms with a hard reality. Namely, that research is power-driven, that requires me at times to abandon the quest for the false conscious position of 'realism'. As a researcher who is not white, over 60, and from an inner-city background, I have not had the luxury to have theories and paradigms named in my honour. So, it is incumbent on me not to forget that I am continuously involved in a struggle for validity as a researcher that tries to maintain my integrity while having a researcher identity shaped by biased an oppressive histories of racism. The interrogation of those factors is enough to justify the need for my use of the bricolage, as I cannot separate any of those aforementioned elements in the claims I make as a researcher. In some respect by accepting the complexity of the world in which I live my response has to also be open, honest, and transparent. For me my 'researcher's imagination' is grounded in epistemological and ontological realities where complexity underpins my recognition of the world in which I live. So much of my life has been presented as deterministic by those who have failed to see, acknowledge, or relate to how history, culture, and race, distorts my lived reality. One dimension of this complexity can be illustrated by the relationship between research and the domain of social theory. Within this researcher's imagination is a desire to attack the complexity of 'academic theorizing', expose the invisible nature of the underpinning power dynamics, and to document the stories and narratives associated with my scholarship. In this process I abandon my quest for peer acceptance, instead focusing on the way I can shape the production and interpretation of the knowledge I produce. I further argue that I can then move out of the world of false consciousness that tells the researcher they are special and into the domain of a researcher who is committed to the liberation and emancipation of the diverse research constituencies. The task of using performance driven research dissemination strategies therefore needs to identify how the researcher can contest, challenge, and overturn privileged research paradigms that keeps communities' hostage to limited access to power and control of their lives.

Becoming a bricoleur

If performance-driven research dissemination means unifying and employing multiple research dissemination approaches such as bricolage then progressive researchers must not strive for neutrality and look beyond upholding the status quo. Having observed the silo mentality that governs so much of what is deemed 'valid' and 'reliable' with relation to research I grew tired of being told it's either this way or that way. My work has always been messy, awkward, challenging, and never linear. What I knew is that by applying standards that didn't quite fit what I was doing, I was constantly in danger of wrecking my work, and more importantly destroying the relationships I had built up with my constituency. A case in point was undertaking some work with young offenders in HMP Wetherby. The project was called 'colours' with the following objective/aims.

Objective

We seek to 'enable' all individuals to represent themselves by fully involving them in ways to become the 'authors of their own lives'. To achieve this, we believe in the values of 'shared experience', by 'embracing diversity', encouraging 'self-expression', and ensuring 'social inclusion via active participation'.

Aims

- To make a difference within our communities by collaborating to provide 'voice', 'influence' and 'opportunities' for those who feel marginalised, disenfranchised invisible, or ignored.
- To enable disadvantaged people to 'participate' more fully in society.
- To affect positive change through 'self-representation'.
- To provide opportunities for increasing personal motivation, supporting mental wellbeing, and improving skills development by raising individual levels of self-belief, motivation, and aspiration.

I had to work in several sites; on the streets, prison, youth centres, and schools. Even though the objective was the same, the data gathering phase was anything but straight forward. Each site required a different approach to engaging, working, and enabling the participants. It was evident that 'one size, did not fit all'. Needless to say, that by operating using a multi-pronged approach I was in a position not only to get the data I needed, but the outcome (a short video) reflected the diversity of perspectives from the participants that could not have happened if I had stuck with the same approach for all the sites I operated in. Although 'bricolage' as an approach to qualitative inquiry, has gained popularity in academic circles, it remains relatively misunderstood, and unpopular, in broader research communities. However, bricolage has many strands within its discipline.

Bricolage dissemination and beyond

Denzin and Lincoln (2000) see 'interpretive bricoleurs' as operating in a critical, multi-perspectival, multi-theoretical, and multi-methodological context. Denzin and Lincoln further see the 'interpretive bricoleur' as someone who 'understands that research is an interactive process shaped by personal history and by those in the setting' (2000: 6). 'Interpretive bricoleurs' similarly recognize that knowledge is never free from subjective positioning or political interpretations, while 'theoretical bricoleurs', work through, and between, multiple theoretical paradigms (Denzin & Lincoln, 2000). The theoretical bricoleur reads widely and is knowledgeable about the many 'interpretive paradigms' that can be brought to any particular problem.

Clearly, Denzin and Lincoln (2000) consider notions of the bricolage to be an approach that enables progressive researchers to engage with the complexity of the meaning-making, the inquiry process, transcending the limitations of 'positivist' approaches that seeks to privilege dominant epistemologies. Kincheloe (2001) suggests that bricoleur researchers engaging with contemporary social theory should have greater awareness of the implicit assumptions within diverse approaches to conducting research and the ways that shape their findings. With this approach Kincheloe further suggests, that bricoleur researchers can make more informed decisions about the nature of epistemological concerns in their field and how to gain a stronger understanding about the worth of the knowledge they themselves produce. Bricoleurs who appreciate of the complexities of the research process should view research methods as involving far more than procedure. When researchers fail to reflect on the unique ways that historical, social, and cultural context generates wider impacts, the outcomes can be reductionist that in turn can lead to a corruption in the understanding of things connected to it (Burbules & Beck, 1999). Connecting the methodological and theoretical aspects of the bricolage helps the researcher act in opposition to social inequality within society. Using the bricolage is an attempt to remove knowledge production and its benefits from the control of elite groups, researchers included. As such, the bricolage is inherently and unapologetically political, dedicated to challenging unequal social relations. Kincheloe (2005) expresses the view that by deploying methodological strategies such as bricolage progressive researchers can offer new solutions to old problems. Again, I return my focus back to my own discipline of criminology. Many criminologists have still not been able to reduce the level of racial disproportionality within the wider criminal justice system (Glynn, 2014). Nor have they been able to stem the tide of violence that is blighting communities around the world (Glynn, 2014). It may be that current approaches to research dissemination ensures that radical and revolutionary ideas are supressed and therefore plays into the hands of those forces who see 'social control' more important than 'social transformation'. If important messages are not getting out there, they cannot equip activists and the wider community with the tools to speak directly to power. Building on Kincheloe (2005) I would like to offer some of my own insights from which to engage in a critical discussion concerning the importance of the deployment of the bricolage:

- **Intersecting contexts**: Knowledge production can never be static and is not an end in itself. We operate in many different social locations, are positioned differently, and are constantly shifting and changing. Therefore, our research needs to respond to those dynamics in ways that are relevant, appropriate, and inclusive.
- **Multiple epistemologies**: Bricoleurs actively seek out diverse epistemologies for their unique insights and sophisticated modes of making meaning. By recognising this epistemological complexity, bricoleurs move beyond their

own cultural context by acknowledging and embracing other ways of seeing and knowing require a multi-pronged approach.

- **Cultural assumptions**: Bricolage actively encourages and pursues complexity, forcing researchers to look at new ways of validating and privileging cultural assumptions that underpin the universality of knowledge production as a whole.
- **Power and knowledge**: Bricoleurs intuitively understand that particular worldviews regarding notions of research rigor, validity and notions of the 'unscientific' at times see some type of research as unworthy of any serious attention. Bricoleurs therefore must be vigilant and at all times remind judgmental researchers that there are many ways to view the same thing, where the outcome may be the same or differ.

The following case study is a small example whereby the use of 'data verbalization' as an expression of the bricolage enabled me to transform a whole classroom.

Case example

I'm in a seminar on research dissemination. A traditional forum where scholars were discussing the pressure they now face regarding 'research impact'. The format for the discussion was predictable; improving PowerPoints, getting into the top academic journals, how to contest neo-liberalism, and on. The sheer level of fear and anxiety generated was not healthy. I decided to speak as I had reached 'panic' overload. I pointed out that maybe the biggest fear was not what they had alluded to previously, but the fear of changing how they do things. I spent a fair amount of time talking about presenting authentically using comedy, music, theatre, spoken work, and music (bricolage). The room lit up. I then expressed the view that if the original research was conducted, ethically approved, and concluded professionally, then the dissemination only had to reflect the key bits of important information. Suddenly, the dynamics in the room changed. The discussion stopped, and I began to run a workshop on alterative and complimentary ways to disseminate research. I concluded with sharing some of my work on 'data verbalization'. That days some lives were changed. The winner overall was using a 'bricolage' approach as a tool for teaching and learning.

Conclusion

The use of bricolage expressed through 'data verbalization' may transcend its original intention/s connected to the expansion of the ways we seek to generate new pedagogies outside of the academy. Using bricolage, we should further gain insights into new modes of thinking, teaching, and learning. In doing so bricoleur researchers can operate much the same as story-makers who operate in participatory, inclusive, and emancipatory ways. To do this bricoleur researchers must also become part of a unified strategy for global north–south concerns. Bricoleur researchers must therefore resist forces of epistemological domination by removing knowledge production and its benefits from the control of elite groups. A key *modus operandi* for bricoleur researchers wanting to position themselves, is to see themselves less as an expert in the field and connect for more to scholar-activism. This position would suggest that the bricoleur researcher must be reflexive at all time, adjusting when personal baggage disconnects from history, society, and culture of others different from ourselves. It is therefore incumbent on all progressive researchers to surrender to the notion that 'one size does not fit all' and epistemological singularity should have no place among researchers who see diversity as the bedrock of positive human relations. Overall, bricolage offers all researchers endless possibilities for change, transformation, alongside recognizing that multi-stranded research dissemination approaches can accommodate the complex nature of modern living.

Summary

This chapter argued for the need to engage researchers in a dialogue that moves research dissemination beyond the confines of the academy using a 'bricolage' approach with relation to the sharing of research data. It further looked at the important role of W.E.B. Du Bois as sociological bricoleur. It concluded by calling for the acknowledgement of the need to develop bricolage and the researcher's imagination, much the same as C. Wright-Mills, the sociological imagination. By envisioning a multi-pronged approach for research dissemination there may be new solutions to old problems that emerge.

Key questions

1. How do you see the use of 'bricolage' approaches to research dissemination within your own work?
2. What are the pros and cons of adopting this approach?
3. What are the consequences of operating with a bricolage approach within your institution?

References

Burbules, N.C. & Beck, R. (1999) Critical thinking and critical pedagogy: Relations, difference, and limits. In: Popkewitz, T.S. & Fendler, L. (eds) *Critical Theories in Education: Changing terrains of knowledge and politics*, London: Routledge.

Denzin, N.K. & Lincoln, Y. (2000) *Handbook of Qualitative Research* (2nd ed.), Thousand Oaks, CA: Sage.

Denzin, N.K. (2010) *The Qualitative Manifesto*, Walnut Creek, CA: Left Coast Press.

Du Bois, W.E.B. (1978) *On Sociology and the Black Community*, Chicago, IL: University of Chicago Press.

Ferrell, J., Hayward, J., & Young, J. (2008) *Cultural Criminology*, London: Sage.

Glynn, M. (2014) *Black Men, Invisibility, and Crime: Towards a critical race theory of desistance*, London: Routledge.

Kincheloe, J. (2001). Describing the bricolage: Conceptualizing a new rigor in qualitative research. *Qualitative Inquiry*, 7(6): 679–692.

Kincheloe, J. (2005) On to the next level: Continuing the conceptualization of the bricolage. *Qualitative Inquiry*, 11(3): 323–350.

Lather, P. (1986) Research as praxis. *Harvard Educational Review*, 56(3): 257–278.

Mills, C.W. (1959) *The Sociological Imagination*, New York: Oxford University Press.

Phillimore, J., Humphries, R., Klaas, F., & Knecht, M. (2016) 'Bricolage: Potential as a conceptual tool for understanding access to welfare in superdiverse neighbourhoods', Iris Working Paper Series. Birmingham, UK: University of Birmingham.

Rogers, M. (2012) Contextualizing theories and practices of bricolage research. *The Qualitative Report*, 17(7): 1–17.

4

CREATING AND PRODUCING DATA VERBALIZATION

'**Data verbalization**?' A term I conceived after seeing the global impact and success of its quantitative cousin '**data visualisation**'. The need to generate a parallel and complimentary revolution around 'performance-driven research dissemination' for qualitative researchers is situated as part of a wider continuum regarding accessible methods associated with presenting challenging and complex research using creative methods such as 'data verbalization'. Currently, there are no major studies, no peer approval, nor do I have any significant claims concerning 'data verbalization' as a critical method of research dissemination. It is in its embryonic phase, designed to engage progressive researchers in a motivational dialogue regarding the way research can be located outside the academy, and rooted within the wider community. 'Data verbalization' is there to be experimented on, played around with, hypothesized, and more importantly developed further with sensitivity and passion. I started with a blank canvas from which to extend the boundaries of research dissemination that would be appropriate for use in today's social media savvy world. The discovery of 'data verbalization' in its subsequent development and expression should be seen more as a complementary aid to any progressive researchers wanting to expand and enhance their repertoire with relation to research dissemination as a whole. In essence this chapter should not be seen as a panacea for research dissemination overall, nor is it a replacement for the countless creative methods and approaches associated with sharing research that have tried and tested histories. It is merely a driver for the intersection of the 'old' and 'new' ways of sharing research using performance-driven techniques in both academic and community settings. I refer to this key driver as the 'Sankofa principle'.

The Sankofa principle

The Sankofa bird is an African mythical creature with its head facing backwards and its feet firmly on the ground. It literally means to 'go back and retrieve'. The

Sankofa bird symbolizes taking from the past what is good and bringing it into the present in order to make positive progress through the benevolent use of knowledge. Essentially, 'data verbalization' utilizes spoken word forms rooted in ancient oral tradition, relocated within a contemporary context in areas such as social media. Important here is in the recognition of how the past informs the future. This requires researchers wanting to engage with 'data verbalization' to avoid negating the power of the oral traditions that underpins its origins and associated techniques. So how did 'data verbalization' actually come about?

Background

As stated previously the genesis for 'data verbalization' emerged out of years of frustration at not being able to find a suitable outlet for disseminating my research back to the constituencies I had collaborated and co-produced with. This state of affairs was partly fuelled by a deeper and more troubling concern. Namely, how could I privilege the stories of the many silent 'voices' of the participants who shared their testimonies with me throughout my many research enquires? Coming from a performance background I had always used creativity as a device from which to bring key research messages to my constituency in accessible and culturally appropriate ways. However, the ongoing struggle to find an infrastructure that would assist myself and other researchers wanting to present the intersection of 'research' and 'performance' for dissemination purposes was, and still is, sadly lacking. For me, I wanted to move research dissemination from a position of merely being an 'add on' to the conclusion of the research process and make it more meaningful and impacting in equal measure. I also wanted to ensure that there was a 'legacy' attached to the work that would become embedded within both the 'social structure' and 'consciousness of the wider community'. I began to talk to friends, colleagues, and those I had co-produced with over the years and was reliably informed that I should not abandon or relinquish my quest to bring performance-driven research dissemination to heightened prominence in academia and more importantly the community. It was further expressed that I should consider integrating my passions for 'storytelling' and 'performed research' by relocating the outcomes outside of the academy. Equally as important was the encouragement from pioneers in the field such as the esteemed Johnny Saldana and ubiquitous Norman Denzin who paved the way for me to build on their own legacies. This chapter therefore introduces the conceptual thinking and processes associated with producing 'data verbalization' stories and details the journey from its inception through to bringing in fruition, citing examples.

The need to tell stories

As a child, I would always fabricate and bend the truth. Fortunately, I had a caring mother and encouraging step-father who pushed me to immerse myself in the world of books that fuelled my imagination. Since then I have worked in variety of story-making and story-telling situations and contexts; workshops, residencies, conferences, and more recently (January 2018) I added a TEDx presentation to my repertoire. To this day, I still extensively use anecdotes and stories in my academic work to break down complex, dense, and abstract ideas/concepts. As modern living is at times fraught with many difficult and confusing challenges there is a need to (re)establish a series of guiding principles and truths by which we can (re)frame our hectic lives. Stories for me are about 'individual' and 'collective memory' that shapes, defines, and understands ontological notions of 'meaning' and 'purpose'. Stories not only bind us together to better comprehend our place in the world, but hand down wisdom through 'word of mouth'. Stories are represented in books, paintings, sculptures, theatre, film, TV, and lately social media. Ultimately, stories are the way we communicate our personal myths, truths, and our more importantly humanity. I wanted to push the boundaries of current research dissemination by envisioning a new landscape which would bring a contemporary 'narrative impact' to communities and other constituencies had previously worked with. At that point I knew I could never look back and had to continue with my quest. In my reflection and after much soul searching I had a significant breakthrough. Inasmuch, as I took a drastic decision: to move my research from the 'page to the stage', and in doing so be committed to bringing the outcomes (and that of other researchers), from the academy to the community.

From page to stage

One of the biggest conflicts I had to face regarding this shift in my focus was having to contend with the orthodoxy who began to challenge and contest how my notion of performing research data would distort or enhance ideas associated with 'reliability' and 'validity'. Babbie (2002) argues that reliability is the consistency of a result over time. Hence quantitative methods are seen as the methods of choice as a result of the controlled environment and the standardization that may arise from testing. Chilisa (2012), on the other hand, supports the view that research methodologies should focus on the concerns and worldviews of the research subjects so that they understand themselves through their own assumptions and perspectives. Mills (1959) similarly argues that researchers should avoid rigid set of procedures and instead seek to develop the 'sociological imagination' that enables the researcher to become a 'craftsperson' using methods much the same as a painter uses colour. Mills further sees that the conventions that governs restrictive research methods can limit envisioning new and improved ways of 'seeing' and 'knowing'. As I began to absorb the emerging binary concerns within the academy I delved deeper into my own motivations for taking a new stance. I refer to this missing link as my 'golden fleece' moment. On two counts. Count one, I wanted to create something that would contest the dominant neo-liberal and neo-positivist research paradigms. Count two, I wanted to push beyond those research lenses that did not address themselves to praxis and wider liberation struggles.

Measurable impact

Equally important was to remind some of my colleagues that raising their profile as researchers or commissioning body was secondary to the measurable impact claims the research purported to make. Denzin (2010) raised my confidence by identifying that the understanding that creative approaches to research dissemination can assist researchers in confronting, engaging with, and working through, the epistemological, methodological, and ethical contradictions and challenges with relation to critical inquiry as a whole. Denzin asks each generation to offer its responses to current and past criticisms. This should force all of us involved in people's lives to become accountable for the choices we make, the findings we seek, and more importantly what we found out. I asked myself another key question: 'For whose benefit is my research?' Understandably, research emerges out a need to create meaning through investigation of social phenomena. This responsibility is mainly entrusted to the academy that is supposed to operate with objectivity, fairness, and have the necessary infrastructure to operate in supportive and meaningful ways. However, for some marginalized and oppressed communities the researcher may need to give them feedback in ways that are accessible, insightful, and will provide some steer as to how to solve a problem, as well as making some sense out of what has happened during the research processes they have been exposed to and engaged with. Many participants I have encountered over the years, especially those in the criminal justice system have expressed reservations about working with 'insensitive researchers' expressing the view that at times they have been 'researched on'. It has also been expressed to me on numerous occasions that at times the methods that were not culturally appropriate, where they were left feeling excluded. The importance of having a (insider) researcher who came from a similar background to their own was often cited as a key component of co-produced research. Of note, the community is a place full of distractions.

Hidden pitfalls

There is never a perfect place to interview, there is also the nature of participants who can at times express doubts, or struggle with their confidence throughout. I am no different from any other researcher who at times approaches research ignorant of some of the hidden pitfalls that lay ahead. However, by being open to scrutiny from those who on the receiving end of the journey of investigation and curiosity I have established a personal code of sensitivity from which to base many of my formative assumptions embedded within the research process itself. Mertens (2007) argues that researchers should be cognizant of the philosophical and political assumptions that guide their work, especially those we work with. Co-constructed research therefore should unify and bring together the researcher and the wider community for mutually agreed aims, objectives, and trajectories for the research that is undertaken. Taking on the role of the researcher can act as a barrier that separates the insider from those in the research setting. As stated previously, the insider positioning views the research process as co-constructions between the researcher and the participants; regard the research participants as 'active informants'; and should attempt to give voice to the informants within the research domain. It is a position that pushed me to develop 'data verbalization', while at the same time reflecting on the understanding of 'research leadership'.

Research leadership

If (human) 'purpose' emerges from a deep emotional and psychological need to find meaning to one's life (ontology), then some of us, like me, discover it through adversity, others through personal discovery, while the power of discernment leads some individuals like myself to a place that demands a personal commitment to see that journey as a 'rite of passage'. Important here is in the interrogation of one's inner motivation for not only seeking but fulfilling one's purpose. However, issues that surrounded my poor socialization and hostile environment created a distraction where I was pushed away from understanding 'why I was here' and 'what I was put here to do'. I had a difficult childhood, a traumatic adolescent growth period, and generally meandered around most of my life searching for a sense of identity that always proved elusive. Yet I have travelled widely, embraced education, read voraciously, culminating in gaining a doctorate, yet still the insecurity and doubt that followed me was constant. It was also true that I had created a family, engaged in community, and had built a large reservoir of friends and associates, and still there my life was predicated with a lack. An interesting point of departure was in my 'age transitions' each decade brought fresh challenges, new thoughts, and was constantly refining my perspectives on life, but plagued with depression, self-doubt, and low self-esteem, I kept looking outward for an explanation. However, I then began to retreat to the confines of my books and started to read the stories of those who had inspired me. They consisted of composers, artists, politicians, philosophers, scientists, and numerous others who had found their true vocation. What emerged answered a question I had been wrestling with for many years. In some respect, the answer had been in front of my face, but I couldn't see it. Writers refer to this state of being as the 'invisible story'. The conflicts between the personal and professional, the spiritual and the social, the intellectual and the philosophical, and lately, doing more or doing less, has provided me with a range of answers which are both exhilarating and fearful in equal measure. By that I mean I had arrived at a place which felt psychologically uncomfortable, but emotionally comforting. I had learned a valuable lesson that purpose is something that happens, a sort of process, which defines the meaning of your life, alongside placing everything else into perspective. To do so I had to be courageous enough to embrace what was happening.

Mobilizing people

Having spent many years working in prisons and the community has taught me valuable lessons on 'mobilizing' people around a key issue or an agenda of some sort. It could be a church pastor rallying the community around an issue that has impacted on people's lives, such as a shooting. On the other hand, it could be a gang member who in a desire to get retribution calls upon the other members of the gang into action. Similarly, I have witnessed community members, those who run local businesses, sports teams' managers, or those who run long-term projects who have the kind of credibility that 'activates' their members into action of some sort. Central to the understanding of activating and mobilizing people into action is in the understanding of how to build 'credibility' as a researcher operating with ethical leadership principles to build, gain, and maintain credibility. 'Credibility' is the glue that binds leader to follower, follower to leader. Credibility like its cousin trust must be earned, built, developed, sustained, and constantly be negotiated. Activating individuals to follow an idea/instruction, change behaviour/structures, or to act on a principle, requires a complex set of negotiations, trust building, and sustained commitment on behalf of the leader. For the activated there is a need to know that the person they are following doesn't exploit, belittle, take for granted, or act in suspicious ways.

Effective research leader

An effective research leader needs to communicate their ideas, strategy, combined with the consequences of the challenges that lie ahead with clarity. A confused research leader will send out mixed messages and could end up misguiding those who are required to make the changes that are required. Failure to consider this will result in sending followers into oblivion. Activating others also requires any research leader to consider the ethical considerations for such actions, especially when those who are signing up to any mission may be risking something both personally or professionally. I myself have had to mobilize many individuals in my role as a theatre director and lecturer. Being both an academic and researcher I have always been concerned about the density of research vernacular, processes, and procedures, combined with the abstract nature of many theoretical ideas. In my work with offenders in particular I have realized the importance of having to 'break down' complex, awkward, or sophisticated concepts so as not to oppress those on the receiving end of any ideas I conveyed. It is incumbent on any research leader to seek out and find relevant, culturally appropriate, innovative and accessible ways to present key research messages down into ways that are suitable for the intended audience. This requires any individual to have a multi-pronged (bricolage) approach. In my case it was, and still is, storytelling. From childhood I grew up on stories as a way of educating myself about life and the things I would face. Those who told me stories understood that storytelling was not just about fun, happy endings, or weaving magic, but one of passing on handed down wisdom that would remain with me for the rest of my life. My mother in parti-cular was a gifted storyteller whose advice I ignored while she was alive, but on her passing, the knowledge has now become the basis of the things I pass on to others. Her anecdotes, metaphors, and general insight to the human condition ensured she passed her legacy onto me. A key to her ability to impart her wisdom and help me understand difficult ideas was in her use of comedy. Mum's comedy was eccentric, colourful, and full of twists and turns, where the ending to the stories was more about my ability to problem solve than it was trying to get a satisfying ending. On reflection what mum taught me was in the understanding of 'audience'. She was as skilled talking to me as her son, as she was talking to a cat or an angry dog. She somehow had a gift of pitching her ideas at the right level regardless of who the audience was. Mum's wisdom formed the basis of my passion for theatre. So much so that for all of my research career, co-producing theatre has underpinned the basis for much of what I do now.

Applied theatre and me

Unable to get my work produced in so-called 'mainstream' theatre, I discovered and embraced 'applied theatre'. Applied theatre is most often undertaken in spaces not usually defined as theatre buildings, with participants who may or may not be skilled in theatre arts and to audiences who have a vested interest in the issue taken up by the performance or are members of the community addressed by the performance. I have used 'applied theatre' in my work in criminal justice, public health, educational, and arts settings. I became involved with applied theatre in the early 1980s when I set up arts-based residencies in prisons. The turning point came in the mid-1980s when I was asked to run a residency with a group of prisoners in a maximum-security prison. This residency called for me to develop 'transformative experiences' for men in prison and in turn use 'applied theatre' as the conduit for personal and collective change. When I began to take a keener interest in research I then became involved with the creation and production of **ethnodrama**.

Ethnodrama

> Ethnodrama consists of dramatized, significant selections of narrative collected through interviews, participant observation field notes, journal entries, and/or print and media artefacts.
>
> *(Saldaña, 2005)*

'Ethnodrama' starts from an 'interpretivist perspective'. That is, it focuses on the meanings that individuals give to their lived experiences (McAdams 1985). 'Ethnodrama' also seeks to enable those same individuals to explore, interpret, and narrate their own story in 'dramatic form'. Denzin (2018) argues that subordinated voices must be heard, helped to speak and that performative social science paradigms may provide some new answers to old problems. In responding to issues of power and inequality Denzin further calls for the construction of counter narratives through the 'dramatization of data'. Ethnodrama, therefore, can be used as an important tool for advocating and promoting action-based learning. This led me further to develop what I refer to as Counter-Narrative Theatre (CNT). CNT is a performative exploration and expression of intersectional counter-narratives using research data

(Glynn, 2014). CNT uses 'dramatized data' to 'challenge' and 'contest' dominant social and cultural assumptions in areas such as public health, criminal justice, and education. It also 'explores' and 'examines' how public, social, and cultural policies might be constructed to eliminate social inequalities. CNT emerged out my doctoral research where the analytical framework I used was Critical Race Theory (CRT). CRT uses storytelling as its analytical framing and operates with two distinct storytelling paradigms. 'Majoritarian stories' told by 'the privileged', and 'counter-stories' told by 'the subordinated' (Solorzano & Yosso, 2002). Generating 'performed counter narratives' brings 'critical theorizing' and marginalized concerns to 'heightened prominence'. The interesting thing about this stage of my development was how impacting the work was. The difficulty however was in the process. It was time consuming, expensive, and required a process that at times was defeated by a lack of significant resourcing. I now needed something more immediate, cost effective that was also contemporary. In 2016, I was invited to a conference in New Orleans (USA) and decided to do something different. I took my conference paper, deconstructed it completely, and created what is now referred to as '**data verbalization**'. I had finally found a way to 'perform' and 'speak' my data.

The birth of data verbalization

In October 2016, I was given a small development grant from Birmingham City University to pilot data verbalization, where I created an experimental space for individuals interested in using the method on their own work. For several weeks, I ran the programme for a diverse group of participants consisting of undergraduates, post graduates, doctoral students, and community members. A series of interactive seminars was used to deliver the key content of the course. Operating as an 'action learning' space the objective is to cultivate a creative community, who could work either independently of collaboratively.

- **Session 1 – Disseminating data**: This session looked at the pros and cons of using disseminating research data.
- **Session 2 – From abstract to premise**: This session focused on developing a 'data verbalization' premise from a journal article abstract.
- **Session 3 – Finding the story**: This session looked at how to turn the 'premise' into the story that will then form the basis of the 'data verbalization' story.
- **Session 4 – Characters and their world**: This session looked critically at the role of 'characterisation' in the 'data verbalization' process.
- **Session 5 – Construction**: This session looked at the process of de-constructing a journal article reading for 'data verbalization' production.
- **Session 6 – From construction to verses**: This session looked at the process of converting generated themes into 'data verbalization' rhymed verses.
- **Session 7 – Producing and staging your data verbalization**: This session looked at the process of producing and staging 'data verbalization' stories.

In the evaluation that followed I captured some critical responses of the participants. The following is a snap shot of what emerged:

MOHAMMED: Initially I thought the challenge would be too great, it was certainly a journey in exploring areas I had not visited before. I gained a brand-new perspective on understanding data and information and translating it for a new audience. I also acquired lots of new skills; rhyming, screen writing, different ways of looking at both narrative and story that went beyond my expectations

REBECCA: What I loved about that process was that we had ample opportunity to test our learning in a supportive group environment. I now know what it is and how to transform data into more creative forms.

MO: The design and structure of the course means that you are interacting and working alongside members of the community, and students having a space to interact has been invaluable.

ALISON: I was exposed to creative areas outside of my experience, which made me aware of the potential of different art forms to disseminate ideas. My preferred medium is writing, and I can envision the translation of my writing into film. I firmly believe that data verbalization would be a useful adjunct to all science and political communication work. As a non-performance person, I was intimidated by most of the exercises we were asked to do but being made to do them was quite liberating.

PEGGY: The data verbalization programme provided theoretical as well as practical support in exploring compilation of stories and alternative modes of communicating research findings. Finally, the diversity of the group (on a range of levels) made the space created an incredibly rich one.

SITARA: My experience with data verbalization encouraged me to step outside of my comfort zone and take a new approach in interpreting and disseminating data specifically tailored to individuals without an academic background. Data verbalization has helped increase my confidence in public speaking and gave me the opportunity to present my ideas confidently to small groups, which I was not familiar with. I gained knowledge of how to pursue different methods of spreading information and was allowed through data verbalization to rebuild my interest in expressing issues through poetry and script writing.

JAMES: I would really like to see a summer school in the future, or an online platform/community where academics, undergraduates, and postgraduates around the world post research in the form of performance to reach the younger generation who are more influenced by social media than a book. The opportunities are endless. I think this would be really different and could bridge the gap between academia and the real world.

SHIRLEY: The 'data verbalization' course offered a range of creative forms from which that data could then be disseminated. I gained a clearer understanding of both the theoretical and practical approach to the 'data verbalization' method, which resulted in me achieving positive outcomes. This course helped to demystify the challenges of accessing overly dense research data. For example, the technique used for breaking down data into manageable amounts, by identifying recurring language helped me to access complicated information.

THASLEEMA: I learned many different skills about how to approach an academic article and making it more enjoyable which I personally never thought was possible!

Analyzing the responses a range of issues emerged that laid the foundation for the philosophy and further development of 'data verbalization' as a viable research dissemination method:

- The process of adaptation
- The inventory
- Ethical considerations
- The process

The process of adaptation

Each stage required careful planning, time management, and resourcing to ensure the smooth running of the process. The first thoughts any researcher should ask themselves is 'what do I bring to the work?' We all have reasons for telling stories, raising awareness, expressing our views, and generally articulating our perspective on the world. However, unless there is a personal (reflexive) questioning of ourselves, we can lose our way and not reach our intended audience. The following inventory is to enable the researcher to firstly seek clarity before embarking on the journey to creating 'data verbalization' stories. The questions are by no means exhaustive and act merely as a guide from which to build a strong initial idea. Many creative people act intuitively in the way they structure their ideas. However, for researchers coming to creativity for the first time or who may not be that confident an inventory provides a safe way from which to begin the process.

The inventory

Location:

- What is the key message/theme of your journal article?
- Is the work to be presented in:
    - A traditional performance space; theatre, lecture hall, etc
    - A social setting; community, public building, etc
    - Open air
    - Site Specific; non-traditional space

Key Considerations:

- Will the outcome be appealing, accessible, and appropriate?
- Will the outcome disseminate the right information?
- Can the work go onto a social media platform?
- Will the outcome maximise community engagement?
- Who are the key stakeholders?
- Is the intended outcome inclusive or exclusive?

Presentation:

- Is it single performer led?
- Is it ritual performance?
- Is it interdisciplinary?
- Does it require scripting?
- Does it require learning?
- Will it require direction?
- Is it multi-media?
- Is it interactive?
- Is it live?
- Is it recorded?

Audience:

- Who is the audience?
- How does your audience consume need to receive information?
- How diverse are the audience/s you are aiming to reach?
- Where and when can I communicate with my audience?
- What are the cultural/social/political considerations when responding to your audience?

Decisions:

- What key decisions does your audience need to make?
- What problems does your audience need solving?
- What does my audience already know?
- What has my audience been told before?
- How will data verbalization assist my audience in making decisions?

The Story:

- What is the story that's being told?
- Whose story is it?
- Why is the story important?

- Why is research required to tell the story?
- What are the considerations required in telling your story?
- Do you need visuals?
- Do you need sound?
- Will you be using comedy?
- Do you need to incorporate movement?
- Do you need to observe cultural conventions?
- Is it a spoken word piece?
- Is it sung?
- Is there an integration between the creative components?
- Is it a call and response piece?
- Is it interactive?
- Is it sensory?
- Will it offend?
- How will you conclude?

On completion of the inventory it is then important to consideration some of the ethical choices bound up in disseminating your research using 'data verbalization'.

Ethical considerations

Ethics are an essential part of the research process, as they set the boundaries between the researcher and the subjects of the inquiry. Similarly, 'data verbalization' is ethically driven from a performance standpoint. The following ethical considerations have been adapted and drawn from the BSC/BSA Ethical Principles:

1. **Copyright**: In the event of using another academics research it is vital that permission to adapt the work into 'data verbalization' should be sought from the relevant institution, publisher, or any other source where the research was published.
2. **Compliance with the law**: Any work undertaken with community members must pay attention to safety and security. Accessing participants in the community requires a sensitive assessment is undertaken to ensure both the researcher and participants can work in a co-produced manner.
3. **Production**: Requires careful handling and will need to be coordinated in conjunction with various community brokers and key contacts.
4. **Obligations to community members**: The rights of community members should be negotiated and brokered throughout. Participation wherever possible should be based on freely given informed consent. All of those involved should be given a release form regarding participating in the study. The release form will contain relevant information about the responsibilities of both the researcher and participants.
5. **Harm reduction**: To reduce the harm to community members, careful consideration will be given to confidentiality and anonymity throughout the development process. If you are addressing or presenting sensitive issues, then

it's vital to assess how the presentation of the idea will be received. Making sure that there are appropriate support mechanisms in place.

6. **Sharing research**: Wherever possible ensure community members are included in all stages of the dissemination processes, as well as being offered the opportunity be part of the performance.

7. **Storage of data**: Data storage and archiving should comply with the requirements of data protection and best practice on confidentiality.

Important here is if you're considering working with another researcher's work, what are the emerging copyright issues? Do you need to obtain permission from co-producers, publishers, or any other source? Overall, the considerations should be looked and addressed prior to starting any adaptation of research data for both 'moral and ethical reasons'. At this stage you should use your inventory to assess the viability of using 'data verbalization' as a method of disseminating your research. It is equally as important to assess your positionality, values, and beliefs. As 'data verbalization' is inherently political any decisions you make regarding the method should not be undertaken likely. We now turn to the '**process of adaptation**'.

The process

- Stage 1 – Finding a premise: Firstly, it is important to generate a 'premise' from which to build your 'data verbalization' story. A premise is the core theme or idea underpinning the article. Usually located within the abstract. The process starts by selecting:

  - A journal article
  - A research report
  - Other data driven source material

Below is a copy of an abstract written for a conference I was attending in New Orleans, in 2017.

Performing desistance: The counter narrative

When looking at Black offenders and their desistance trajectories, whose narrative do we privilege? Desistance is increasingly conceptualized as a theoretical construct used to explain how offenders orient themselves away from committing crimes. However, to date there has been little work undertaken to examine how notions of 'race, racialization, and intersectionality' enhances or impedes the desistance trajectories as told by Black offenders themselves. While racialization centres on the social meaning attached to 'race', intersectionality understands that human beings are shaped by the interaction of different social locations through a series of connected systems and structures of power, where independent forms of privilege and oppression are created. This paper calls for the development of 'counter-narrative theatre' (CNT) as a performative expression that provides a narrative space for Black offenders to 'tell their own stories' as both the 'experts' and 'knowers' of lived reality with relation to their criminality. It concludes by arguing that this 'performed desistance narrative' must both contest and transcend 'criminological race neutrality' and in doing so privilege the narrative of Black offenders with relation to our understanding of crime as a whole. Having read the abstract many times I eventually extracted the core theme that underpinned the paper:

'performative expression provides a narrative space for black offender's to tell their own stories'.

Now I had identified the premise behind my 'data verbalization' story I could begin to identify those themes within my paper that connected itself to the overall premise. Much the same as undertaking a literature review that addresses itself to the research question, a story premise works in the same way. The premise is the guiding principle that forms the foundation of the 'data verbalization' story. In essence if the story you're telling works effectively, then the audience will understand the premise that underpins the narrative.

- Stage 2 – Highlighting: Once you have your premise read your article many times over to internalise the story of the article. On becoming familiar with the overall narrative drive of the article, highlight key phrases/important words much the same as you would do when undertaking 'thematic analysis' or 'grounded theory'. On completion of this exercise transfer the highlighted information to index cards and group them into categories. Structure your phrases and words into codes and categories by laying the cards out in front of you. In doing so you can begin to restructure the card that building into a story. As academic journal articles are full of ideas that flow in a linear fashion, it is important in the adaptation you observe the rules of storytelling, by creating a story that has a clear beginning, middle, and end.
- Stage 3 – Rhymes: Using rhyme is the most rewarding part of writing any lyric, but the most frustrating if it doesn't work. To write rhyme well takes practice. The careful use of the right word at the right time can make or break a piece of work. To avoid forced rhyming (rhyme made because you can't find the right word to match another) use the following to assist you:

  - Dictionary
  - Thesaurus
  - Rhyming dictionary

Remember some golden rules before you embark on using rhyme:

- Rhyme is a science all of its own. Study every form.
- Read and learn from the work of others.
- Don't be lazy. Use words/rhymes wisely.
- Why swear if you can use a better word?
- Be critical of your work.

- Learn how to edit rhymes.
- Break the rules once you know them.
- Don't be too clever. Make the rhyme suit the form.
- Let it go if it's not working.
- Be economical with your rhymes.

As you now have a premise, a range of sentences/words, arranged themes, and a basic narrative structure, you can then begin the task of generating rhymes to accompany the 'data verbalization' story. This phase requires a significant amount of rewriting resulting in many redrafts, until you have the final draft. It is vital that you create rhyming patters that flow and are consistent.

- Stage 4 – Studio recording:

Case example – Silenced (2017)

This case example looks at the concluding phase of the data verbalization. Namely, translating the written adaptation into a recorded 'data verbalization' story. As stated previously I was about to present a paper in New Orleans and wanted to do something different. Again, I had grown tired of the predictable format for conference presentations; a chair, four presenters, each with 20 minutes each, complete with a plenary. I wanted to do something different. So, I deconstructed my paper, selected key phrases, and repositioned the selections into a different narrative structure. I then took a detour and decided to make the whole piece rhyme. When I finished the adaptation from academic paper to a spoken word piece, it went from 8000 words, down to 2000, was much punchier, and lost none of its impact. I then made my way down to a local recording studio and worked with a team of hip-hop producers who produced a beat comprising a jazz sample, drum machine loops, and some original piano solos. The result was amazing. So much so that radio stations began to take a keen interest. And the rest they say is history. The following is a breakdown of how the process works:

- **Composition**: Working with a music producer means relinquishing elements of the overall control of the process at this moment in time. Whereas in the beginning of the process you are the sole author of the piece, it now becomes part of a collaborative enterprise. This next phase of the process is about composing and producing music that moves the work from the page and eventually onto the stage. Rather than use traditional questionnaires, interviews, focus groups, the use of music as an integral part of 'data verbalization' methodology provide an infinite number of possibilities to connect the adapted research to a wider audience.
- **Finding the premise**: The producer first listens to the adapted material minus any music. In doing so the producer can assess the required tone and cadence of the piece overall. This is then followed by the scoping of a range of musical ideas. I have always used jazz/reggae merged with hip-hop drum

beats as they are accessible, popular, and have a proven track record when it comes to audiences. At this stage both the producer and myself listen to the emotion, rhythm, movement, and timing that balances and complements the voice of the orator. I tend to perform my own work. In other cases, you may decide to get another performer or actors to voice it for you. Once both myself and the producer are happy with the musical choices it's time for the producer to work independently.

- **Sampling, chops, time stretching, grooves**: The production team then spend hours going through jazz/blues music, which is then used to sample the initial music track. Sampling is a process used in the music industry where a small amount of an already produced piece of music can be extracted to lay the foundation for other recorded tracks. The sampling equipment is a creative beat making with an acclaimed live sounds and sound library. It is used to create and perform rhythms, harmonies, and melodies, for the track 'Silenced' and keeps you laser-focused on the quest for the perfect groove. Within a pattern-based sequencer and high-performance sampler and exemplary drum synths samples. Machine studio redefines hands-on control, which we use in waveforms, patterns, and scenes, to chop and stretch the sounds and instruments we needed for my first 'data verbalization' track 'Silenced'. This hardware sampler used inputs music files of the jazz song where appropriate section of the original music are selected.
- **Making the drum beat and patterns**: Let's take the most basics; mostly every tune has a kick drumbeat, which defines its rhythm. Beats come in groups of four that are called bars the first beat of every bar is usually stressed to make it distinguishable from the other three. The bars are in turn grouped into 4 and 8 chunks called phrases for example 4-bar phrase has 16 beats. Phrases are of key importance when you which consists parts of intro and verses with phrase changes of an even number every 16 bars, where most normal tracks have intro verse and chorus and consist of an even number of 4 bar phrases with regular intervals that normally equal to one or two, 8 bar chunks.
- **Arranging of the track**: The song structure of 'Silenced'; drum kick, snare, clap, and sampled piano chords sampled to create a hook for the track. This is then followed by inputting actual piano sounds to that complement the musical phrase changes. The importance of this process is the working on the relationship between the words and music, to create a blended piece where one element doesn't dominate the other. In essence, the arrangement is a digital version of classical composition. It is the process that brings the finished track to life emphasizing the nuances within both the linguistic and musical elements of the piece overall.
- **Voicing the track**: Before I could voice the track, I am sent a version to listen to, practice, and immerse myself fully in what the producer has created. Working in a recording studio requires me to develop skills of micro-phone techniques associated digital recording. The microphone is very sensitive and will pick up any sound. Hence the need to practice avoiding doing several

major takes. I also learned that it is easier to use a computer to read my work, acting very the same as a tele prompter on TV. Holding paper to read your work can result in 'paper shake', which can be an inhibiting aspect of studio recording.

- **Mastering for release**: Mastering is the final stage before releasing the track, which is the final technical and complex music production process, within the confines of a very accurate studio environment (acoustically and in terms of reference grade, full spectrum high resolution monitoring). Its goals are sonic corrections though use of equalizers and dynamic control, enhancements, volume balancing, decision making relative to perceived volume, sequencing and spacing of tracks, final quality control now that I had recorded the vocals. The next stage is to release the completed track on all media platforms which will be discussed later in this book.

Silenced – Data verbalization story

Below is the finished piece (available on ITunes, Amazon, and Spotify).

Silenced

Ever since the fate of African peoples was debated, signed, sealed 'N' decided
Their descendants have been enslaved, oppressed, scattered, vilified 'N' derided
Many White historians have made claims using methods that are poorly analytical
'N' many Black scholars have tried to make the agenda much blacker 'N' more political
'N' in spite of all the research that's been funded, carried out, tested 'N' conducted
The 'race 'n' crime' debate falls on deaf ears 'N' is badly negated 'N' corrupted
Whilst the privileged elite ignore their implicit bias, necessary changes are overtly resisted
As the machinery of control 'N' risk by the corporate world is privatised 'N' duly enlisted

Discussing racial disparity 'N' criminal justice in academia is hardly ever shared
This omission can no longer be tolerated 'N' must be challenged 'N' must be aired
We need a new lens to view the issues that must be made visible 'N' brought to the fore
'N' focus less on the symptoms of inequalities 'N' focus more on the core
Desistance explains how offenders come 'off the road' 'N' terminate their offending
'N' yet mass incarceration for black people as a whole is growing 'N' never ending
Whilst Intersectionality talks about different social locations connected to systems of power
The criminal justice system's racialized motto screams 'to control, oppress' 'N' 'devour'

How do we erode institutional power that maintains 'N' sustains racist policies 'N' practice?

How do we address the systemic contexts that oppress, control by turning bias on its axis?

How can black offenders cease offending if their dreams are not embraced 'N' supported?

How can they tell their own stories if their voices are always silenced 'N' always thwarted?

How do they begin to see a future when 'colour blind' research is an academic norm?

When statistics obscure the lived reality of 'race' using methods that are tired 'N' worn

How then can black offenders experience meaningful 'N' productive reintegration?

If ideas that are supposed to assist them increases not reduces their racial subordination

Desistance for Black offenders requires pushing forward racial justice goals 'N' needs

Provide insights 'N' contexts 'N' expose how the criminal system consumes 'N' feeds

It should then generate a 'counter narrative' telling stories of Black resistance

That will create a pathway 'N' a transition towards their re-entry 'N' their desistance

Black scholars must contest 'N' remove systems of inequality 'N' racialized subordination

To do so requires what Garvey did, some unified collective politicised coordination

This counter narrative must move beyond mere descriptive accounts of black oppression

Where the emerging truths become a tipping point for action, transition 'N' progression

How can black offenders be effectively worked with 'N' be properly rehabilitated?

How can we stop the moral panic when right realists want black offenders annihilated?

How can intersectional processes in criminal justice systems be better understood?

How can disparities be addressed improving things for everyone's greater good?

How can rehabilitative processes engage black offenders when they are context dependent?

If their desistance is impeded by a system that offers them nothing remotely transcendent

How do they re-enter from prison when there are major obstacles to staying 'crime free'?

When the racialisation of the 'social structure' turns the lock 'N' then throws away the key

To successfully desist black offenders need to return back to their home communities

Where both sides are brought together to explore mutual benefits 'N' real opportunities

Work needs to be done to help them understand about the victims they have affected

Using restorative means, building social capital, where they are relocated 'N' re-connected

Where efforts are made to create meaningful opportunities that will support 'N' engage

Hopes 'N' dreams that will enable them to have a second chance 'N' turn a new page

Where they will be able propel themselves creating the pathways enabling them to desist

Otherwise their bid for freedom will be taken away, as the criminal justice system will insist

As many black offenders threaten the social order that protects the interest of the elite
Opposition to this must be constant 'N' must lay blame firmly at the system's feet
Desistance must include a new way to improve black self-concept 'N' increase racial
pride
Whilst defective theoretical ideas must be driven out 'N' exposed with nowhere to hide
Black mass incarceration must be reframed within a new political 'N' historical frame
Where notions of control, power 'N' privilege are cast out, never to linger or to remain
Whilst intersectionality should include 'N' transcend the binary opposition of 'race'
To show how a truer reflection of the black experience of justice can take its right place

What should this paradigm shift consist of, talk about, look like, contain, 'N' entail?
How will this position bring about change 'N' transformation 'N' ultimately 'lift the
veil?'
This revision must envision foregrounding black offender's desistance aspirations
'N' examine how racism 'N' White privilege are impacting on many black
generations
The intersection of crime 'N' 'racialisation' needs to be better understood 'N' explained
Whilst poor research should be exposed, brought to account, named 'N' then shamed
We need to defend the infringed civil 'N' human rights of black offenders as a whole
Whilst challenging traditional theories by questioning their elitist 'N' privileged role

We must ensure that the counter-narrative of black offenders is given real prominence
It needs to be pragmatic, assertive, 'N' told using culturally competent common sense
We must necessitate 'N' encourage black offenders to transcend all of their silence
'N' recognise racial privilege as a form of psychic lynching or plain old 'racist violence'
We must further challenge the dominant discourse on racialisation within criminology
'N' demand racial reform within the criminal justice system without fear or apology
We must oppose dominant meanings in relation to social change 'N' power relations
'N' fight against house slaves in the master's house wanting acceptance 'N' assimilation

We must provide a new lens to analyse how racism reproduces broader social patterns
'N' how the racialisation of the criminal justice system creates its trends 'N' fashions
We must raise the profile of black criminological theorising about crime as a whole
Start a different conversation, putting Uncle Tom scholars on probation 'n' on parole
We must embrace 'N' include unified perspectives that enable black offenders to desist
'N' move beyond philosophies 'N' theories that fabricates 'N' focuses purely on the risk
Malcolm X's wisdom stated 'you're either part of the problem or part of the solution'
So where do you stand, what's your position, what will be your contribution?
We can no longer be bound by other people's notions 'N' definition of how we see race

We can no longer allow our thoughts, dreams, 'N' our ideas to disappear without trace
We can no longer allow ideas about race, crime, 'N' justice to be shaped by presumption
We can no longer embrace an agenda owned 'N' run by White privileged consumption
We can no longer listen 'N' praise White or Black lies, myths 'N' unrealistic illusions

> We can no longer operate with false consciousness, distractions 'N' have no solutions
> We can no longer tolerate, conceal, hide 'N' be speaking everyone else's truth
> We can no longer ignore the conspiracy, when we have the evidence 'N' certainly the proof
> Ever since the fate of African peoples was debated, signed, sealed 'N' decided
> Their descendants have been enslaved, oppressed, scattered, vilified 'N' derided
> We must push our truths out, crush the insults, destroy the deceit 'N' the lies
> Scholars must be committed to racial justice, without fear, without compromise
> The system of justice that has failed black offenders 'N' Black people is criminal
> Through slavery, colonialism, into modern times the changes have been minimal
> The time is now to present a 'counter narrative' that will inspire, revolutionise 'N' resist
> If the lessons from the past aren't learnt, the opportunity for change will be missed.
>
> *(Glynn, 2018)*

Having presented 'silenced' several times in conferences, community venues, radio, and various social media platforms, the impact varies according to the medium. However, what is unmistakable is the immediacy of presenting research this way. Academics and non-academic alike garner different things from the subject matter and style of presentation, creating the context for immediate feedback and discussion. In doing so the immediacy creates 'dialogue' between groups that wouldn't normally meet or converge. It is also true that the rendition of 'data verbalization' stories such as 'silenced' can create an event type atmosphere, where spoken word, rap, and grime artists will seize the moment to present their own issues or a counter narrative of their own. In doing so 'data verbalization' becomes a catalyst for collaborative voices to participate in a shared dialogue in a space that is open and democratic.

Final thought

A ritual is the enactment of a myth, and myths are stories of our search through the ages for truth, meaning, and significance. We all need to tell and understand our story. When we make no provision for the passing on of those myths, many people will create their own. For those researchers who fit the criteria, negotiate the terrain, and allow themselves to be compromised for the sake of peer review publications, things are fine. For the researchers who are relegated to the margins, and represent research not considered part of the mainstream dialogue, there is a major problem of denied access, promotion and distribution of important ideas. The lack of recognition afforded to some researchers who have a different point of view of the world creates anguish and frustration, that needs to channelled in a pro-active and productive manner using methods such as 'data verbalization'. All too often the cries from marginalized researchers are:

1. The lack of opportunity to share political, challenging, and controversial ideas.
2. A strong feeling of exclusion from the so-called mainstream academic agenda.
3. A sense of constant isolation from other progressive researchers.

4. No real infrastructure for the progressive researchers to come together, net-work, and share ideas.
5. Little or no access to the world of creative research dissemination development.

Working, as a researcher in today's neo-liberal landscape is fraught with as many problems as there are benefits. Generating work; having to be your own marketer; the endless round of funding deadlines; and so on, all eat into valuable creative time. Researchers are equally supposed to research, lecture, write, alongside being a businessperson, administrator, negotiator, pitcher of ideas. Making headway through the murky world of peer review is bad enough, but without a clear, focussed, and strategic approach in occupying the market place, a lot of researchers are destined to rendered invisible with piles of ideas languishing on shelves and occupying space within cupboards. For many researchers the issue of representation of their research, occupying the so-called market place, and generating 'reach and impact' is fraught with many problems. If researchers are isolated from each other where the support networks are fragmented, seldom connect with each other, then word of mouth, and other uncoordinated pockets of creativity, to generate work can be the only options. If you're not part of those networks, in the know, or living away from nucleus of activity, it seriously restricts promoting important work. In areas such as prisons, health, education, there are networks with varying degrees of specialist knowledge that respond to the needs of that particular market, but they usually patchy, have a limited reach, and are small in profile. There needs to be a way for progressive researchers to distribute their work which is run as a cooperative, which is self-determined in ethos. When one surveys the terrain of progressive researchers there is no doubt some great stuff taking place. However, it is my view that energies can be better spent by not responding or reacting to the dictates of the 'peer review' system or 'institutional cherry picking'.

Summary

This chapter looked at the evolution and development of 'data verbalization' as a method of research dissemination. Important here was to explore my journey from ethnodrama to data verbalization, and how this led to the development of the actual processes involved. It concluded by arguing the need for data ver-balization to create new insight and understanding through which to assess those factors and processes that would enhance communities' ability to improve their engagement with, and connection to, wider public and social policy concerns, whilst at the same time shaping how those policies are designed and delivered using fresh approaches to research dissemination.

Reflective questions

1. How important is exploring new ways to disseminate research data creatively?
2. What role could 'data verbalization' play in disseminating your own research?

References

Babbie, E. (2002) *The Basics of Social Research*, Belmont, CA: Wadsworth Publishing.

Chilisa, B. (2012) *Indigenous Research Methodologies*, London: Sage.

Denzin, N.K. (2010) *The Qualitative Manifesto*, Walnut Creek, CA: Left Coast Press.

Denzin, N.K. (2018) *Performance Autoethnography: Critical pedagogy and the politics of culture*, London: Sage.

Glynn, M. (2014) *Black Men, Invisibility, and Crime: Towards a critical race theory of desistance*, London: Routledge.

Glynn, M. (2016) 'Platform "Data Verbalization Lab" Creative Dissemination of Research Data', *Journal to the Stage (Project Report)*, Birmingham, UK: Birmingham City University.

Glynn, M. (2018) *Silenced Data Verbalization Track*, Birmingham, UK: Natural and Secret.

McAdams, D. (1985) Power, Intimacy, and the Life Story, London: Guilford Press.

Mertens, D. (2007) 'Transformative paradigm: Mixed methods and social justice', *Journal of Mixed Methods Research*, 1(3): 212–225.

Mills, C.W. (1959) *The Sociological Imagination*, New York: Oxford University Press.

Saldaña, J. (Ed.) (2005) *Ethnodrama: An anthology of reality theatre*. Walnut Creek, CA: Alta-Mira Press.

Solorzano, D. & Yosso, T. (2002) 'Critical race methodology: Counter storytelling as an analytical framework', *Qualitative Inquiry*, 8(1): 23–44.

5

DATA VERBALIZATION AND IMPACT

This position chapter focuses on the contentious issue of 'reach' versus 'impact' with relation to research dissemination. Research impact is seen as a way of measuring the social, cultural, or political significance of the research undertaken, the amount of income generated, or how the outcomes have generated change. However, there are many types of 'impact' that can be best understood away from pure scientific terms. For example, epistemologically, indigenous communities may navigate the social world using ancestral connections that culturally transcend the need for rationality in examining the social world. It is also important to reflect on how the intersectional dynamics within research 'enhances' or 'impedes' overall research impacts if they are not overtly embedded in the overall research design. Research is also full of complex, contradictory, and layers of power, which may at times generate impacts that are negative and obstructive. For those communities who have been impacted in this way, the outcomes of research can be devastating or at worse carry adverse outcomes. Here I would like to add a reflection on my own experience of victimhood regarding poorly constructed research. In the late 1970s, I was a participant in a research enquiry centring on education of black boys in schools and exclusions. A research team employed by the local authority I resided in comprised all white people, had little or no connection to the community, and operated with insensitivity and impunity. In some respect, it had shades of street level bureaucracy (Lipsky, 1968). Street-level bureaucracy is where local operatives have direct contact with members of the general public and carry out and/or enforce the actions required by government. The outcome of the research became reductionist in responding to the issues under investigation. The resulting outcome galvanized community action against the local authority who faced an on-going battle with those of us who felt that a process designed to assist the exclusion of a significant section of the community from schools, became tainted by an ill-equipped research team. I further contend that important information that emerges from research should be disseminated in ways that are accessible, relevant, and strive for 'impacts' grounded in ways that are culturally competent. This in my view connects the researcher directly to the subject's community of the research enquiry itself, thus reinforcing the importance of 'co-constructed' activities ranging from inception to conclusion of the research process. In doing so, research impact becomes an affirming experience, with shared outcomes. So, what is research impact?

What is impact?

As a qualitative researcher I know that many impact standards are very clearly defined and benchmarked according to quantitative standards. This in itself can and does create significant problems when the expectation on 'impact' is firmly rooted in institutional desires and contexts that are at times exclusive, not inclusive. For me, 'impact' at times is applied by institutions as the effect/s as intended by policy makers and programme planners, intended beneficiaries, and other vested interests. As both an ethnographer and a social justice campaigner; whether attempting to 'speak to power' or seeking permission to look at things that hurt and oppress people is always loaded down with the kind of academic baggage that at times, forces a retreat away from the communities I engage with. I take this position based on observing and at times colluding with the exploitative role we operate at times in order to gather data, without considering how our work will be received, translated, and acted upon. Equally as important is in the recognition that some communities commission research and evaluations independently of the academy and set a different agenda that researchers must respect and adhere to. The restriction and exclusion around my work as a critical race scholar with specific reference to my work on 'race and crime', forced me to turn to for support from the very same communities in which I conducted the research. I needed assistance in bringing my research to the wider public that was at times being hindered by academic bureaucracy. It was my contention at the time that applying a white privileged position to my research, not only did it render the outcomes of my work invisible, but it also played a part in ensuring my work was not considered mainstream enough. For me it was very much a form of academic colonization where I had to adopt the institutional way of doing things or my hard work scored no value. By using an arts-based approach such as 'data verbalization' I began to address and contest dominant dissemination paradigms and begin to chart a new path that was no less valid, but more importantly much more culturally relevant, as will be explored later in this chapter. So, what are research impacts?

What are research impacts?

Arts Council (2006) argue that the arts have a positive impact on the people who engage with them. They further argue that there is mounting evidence that the arts, particularly contemporary practices, have a distinctive and important, but under-realized role in delivering access and social inclusion across society. To demonstrate the arts can contribute to the achievement of wider social objectives is an on-going dilemma for researcher, practitioners, and politicians alike. However, using arts-based approaches when disseminating research creates some interesting possibilities. Namely, as academics we have been gifted with tools of analysis, critical thinking, and active theorizing, that gives us epistemological space to envision future possibilities. Beckett (2000) Cabinet Office's Initiative Modernizing Government made the following recommendations:

- Openness needs to be a pro-active strategy built into a planned structure for collecting and disseminating information.
- Effective public/private sector partnerships can deliver complex messages across diverse sectors of the economy.
- The Internet has the potential to lead the future delivery of communications.

The above recommendations clearly set out a position for how the Government sees the need for multi-faceted approaches to message dissemination and measurement. Integral to any such approach should be the inclusion of frameworks and paradigms that operate within a range of culturally relevant and appropriate contexts/situations. Although research impacts are vitally important, the privileging of one form of assessment over another could lead to marginalizing valuable insights-based on a form of explicit bias, designed to reinforce and uphold existing social divisions. I see research impact primarily as a moment of influence on the local infrastructure emerging from my academic work, shaped by co-constructions of research with individuals and communities engaging in collective social change and transformation. As much academic impact tends to focus on a culture of 'citation indicators', 'peer reviews', or 'knowledge transfers' tied to vested interests. In itself it is not a problem, but research peers sharing with peers, not only preaches to the converted, but it also can become a breeding ground for unnecessary researcher competition. I still believe in good old fashion 'curiosity' and 'discovery' to drive my research. It is indeed my observation and experience that some definitions of research impact as it is currently posited in my institution does little to broaden the appeal of research within the communities in which they serve. I feel extremely passionate about the need for progressive researchers to immerse themselves in a community context, and to operate ethically using cultural sensitivity at all times. Critical care and attention should be paid to all aspects of culture, faith, language, values, and beliefs operating as guiding values. In doing so this should form the basis in which our engagement and participation is driven in the communities we serve.

Accountability

By serve, I mean we are not passive observers to the life of others, but part of a wider continuum for social justice, where we have a clearly defined role. In essence, the research in itself cannot be the sole basis of how impact is measured. Our work should be accountable to, and engage with, those cultural norms, as a way of gaining, building, and sustaining trust, in the communities that the research is designed to affect. In my field of criminology, I have had much of my work taken out of context or relegated to the category of academic identity politics. Yet those same well-intentioned metrics that critique my work can only go so far. In short, biased and inappropriate metrics or mono-cultural indicators of how well my work has been received or impacted, at times struggle to inform communities concretely as to what the outcome of the research influence was. I do not know and cannot know everything about the mechanisms by which academic research influences other researchers or impacts on external audiences. However, I want to know, and do not want to stray into the world of bending my research to suit agendas, or to merely deliver what my university colleagues or funders want to hear. Our job as researchers is not to just put ideas and findings out there in those comfortable and predictable formats, waiting passively for the next star rating in an academic journal. The responsibility of all researchers should be to envision a wider and more impacting outcome that not just informs, guides, and motivates the consumers of our hard work, but to speak, deconstruct, and dismantle, those structures that oppress, where research becomes the powder for the musket. Ensuring critical research is presented creatively combined with contributing to the social world where the researcher is embedded should be a clear and overt destination. To do so requires progressive researchers to search their conscience, evaluate their position, and then operate without fear or suspicion. In essence the 'proof of the pudding' is less rooted in what the institutional need is, but more of the gateways that are created to generate significant impact.

Proof of the pudding

When one thinks of research dissemination, hip-hop artist Jay Z, and reggae icon Bob Marley don't automatically spring to mind. However, through the creative expression of their ideas, both artists have sold millions of albums (reach) alongside changing much of the face of popular culture (impact). How then does the symbiotic relationship between 'reach' and 'impact' increase 'academic capital' using performance driven data dissemination methods such as 'data verbalization'? From its inception 'data verbalization' stories put to music and staged live, have amassed global audiences when placed on social media platforms such as ITunes, Deezer, Sound Cloud, Twitter, Facebook, WhatsApp, LinkedIn, and Instagram. Similarly, 'data verbalization' performed live in front of audiences has generated insights and understanding that has clear cultural and emotional impact. In my work in the community and prisons, many community members I have talked to at times have felt excluded from the research process when they feel they are seen as merely a repository for a tested hypothesis. That is my view is not the fault of research, but bad research. From its inception data verbalization aimed to create a sensory experience to provide the audience with an accessible way of interpreting the data that is also entertaining. I am sure there are many researchers who would wince at the thought of seeing their work as entertaining. However, when presenting research around controversial or challenging issues, sensitive dissemination presented openly can provide stimulus for discussion, dialogue, and shared communication. Using dissemination as a tool for 'safe' dialogue, when other methods generate fear or upset should also be an embodied part of the research process as a whole.

To the doubters and well poisoners

'Data verbalization' has now generated an infinite number of possibilities to generate significant reach and impact, alongside building an audience of followers who can access the work through phones, screens, and headphones. There will no doubt be the traditionalists who will pour scorn and hate the thought of social media playing such a role in bringing research data to the masses. However, at a time of fake news and lack of access to research distribution outlets, these mediums provide critical researchers and scholar activists a platform from which to talk directly to those who need to hear the messages contained within the original research itself. It is therefore important to reframe the lens when examining the impact of 'data verbalization'. Using an 'artistic', not traditional 'academic' lens is required based on how notions of 'impact' are constructed. I argue that much disseminated research can and does communicate itself to satisfy mainly funders, peers, and other vested interests and elitist power structures. However, research that reflects oppressed and marginalized communities can require different epistemological and ontological concerns of that research constituency, not just in terms of gathering the data, but in how the findings are distributed, consumed, and processed. In doing so, this requires dissemination of ideas that addresses and matches those concerns that may operate much the same as theatre in education or other forms of creativity associated with liberatory goals. So, what is impact? Why is it important in research? And more importantly what does 'data verbalization' have to offer researchers? A further questioning would suggest there is a gap within the way claims regarding impact are looked at, measured, or even understood, in communities who are excluded from dissemination process. This position would suggest there is an 'impact cul-de-sac'.

A new lens required

If there is such a thing as an 'impact cul-de-sac' it is important to look at why? My own position on this issue centres on how we as researchers operate within a culturally sensitive and competent positionality. I am proposing that 'intersectionality' is a more appropriate lens from which to locate and contextualize how we disseminate our work in communities. To date there has been little work undertaken to examine how the 'intersections' of race, class, and gender impacts on sharing/distribution of research data in marginalized communities. As a Critical Race scholar, it is also increasingly apparent that 'race' as a singular category of 'social inequality' does not adequately explain the multiple oppressions that many communities face. Intersectionality is an understanding of human beings as shaped by the interaction of different social locations. These interactions occur within a context of connected systems and structure of power. Through such processes, independent forms of privilege and oppression are created. In my own discipline of criminology Covington (1995) argues that the reproduction of knowledge about crime is 'cultural' in terms of 'questions asked', 'comparisons made', and 'hypothesises tested'.

Check ya privilege

Currently, the landscape that underpins much of the research and theorizing around 'race and the racialization of crime' tends to be located within a range of 'social contexts' and 'situations'. Through such systems and structures independent forms of privilege and oppression are created, maintained, and sustained. Burgess-Proctor (2006) argues that the future of feminist criminology lies in the willingness to embrace intersectionality as a theoretical framework as it recognizes multiple intersecting inequalities. Similarly, I argue that using an 'intersectional frame' of reference would provide a stronger context to examine those factors that either 'enhance' or 'impede' many contemporary problems within our communities. Barak et al (2001 also argue that notions of intersectionality not only describe an individual's experience of the world, but more importantly understanding the symbiotic relationship between race, class, and gender is required in order to fully understand the social world in its widest context. It may be that the current framing of race, class, and gender operating as independent variables should use a more critical lens such as intersectionality when looking at research overall. This in my view would enable 'intersectional' ways of 'seeing' and 'knowing' as deepening our understanding of how oppressions are generated, reproduced, and maintained. Glynn (2014), on the other hand, points out that unless we view the mechanisms behind social inequality using an 'intersectional' frame, the deeper understanding of the current status of black people in general will continue to be rendered invisible, null, and void. Ridgeway concludes by positing that it is status that drives group differences as organizing axes of inequality, and then the acknowledgement of the cumulative elements of group inequality as put forward by notions of intersectionality must inform contemporary analysis of the problems and issues arising. Ridgeway's view has implications for the study of black offenders. Choo and Ferree (2010) argue that intersectionality places marginalized groups at the centre of the research process. They further argue that intersectionality as a process sees power as relational, hence drawing attention to subordinate groups with relation to power and privilege in society. I similarly call on all progressive researchers to use an intersectional approach that draws on the cultural knowledge and lived experience of community members in the design, collection, and interpretation of data where the understanding of their 'worldview' and the 'social context' they operate in will shed light on a wider distribution of social inequality.

Rendered invisible

Glynn (2014) identified that the social, political, and historical experiences of black offenders has been largely absent within criminal justice policy and much of criminological theorizing. Glynn further argues that this omission distorts and does not reveal the full extent of the problems black offenders' face, when having positive outcomes while coming into contact with the criminal justice system as a whole. Freire (1970) points out that the oppressed are better placed at times to understand their oppression, and argues their voices must speak and be heard. Denzin (2010) similarly points out that for 'subordinated and oppressed voices' to be heard, they must be assisted in their desire to 'transcend their silences'. It is hoped that by using intersectional approaches when conducting enquiries we will be able to lead toward eradicating multiple oppressions faced by so many sections of the offender populations and the communities they come from. For researchers to actualize cultural sensitivity with the dissemination process to increase 'impact potential', I am further calling for all of us to expand our ethical frameworks that govern much of what we do to anchor it firmly within a culturally competent framework.

Cultural competence

> Cultural competence is defined as a set of behaviours, attitudes, and policies that come together in a system, agency, or among professionals and enables that system, agency, or those professionals to work effectively in cross–cultural situations.
>
> *(Isaacs & Benjamin, 1991)*

Being culturally competent means having the capacity to function effectively in other cultural contexts. Essentially, many young people within their respective peer groups develop shared values, ideals, dreams, etc., that bond them through social interaction and the transmission of their various cultural experiences. Together they develop a level of 'cultural and social competence'. For researchers to complement their engagement with, and delivery to, communities they strive toward the development and creation of processes that are 'culturally competent'. The National Centre for Cultural Competence in Georgetown (USA) cites five essential elements that contribute to a system's ability to become more culturally competent:

1. Value diversity: Valuing diversity means accepting and respecting differences.
2. Cultural self-assessment: Through cultural self–assessment processes, services are better able to see how their actions affect people from other cultures.
3. Dynamics of cultural interactions: An on-going evaluation investigating the many factors that can affect cross–cultural interactions.
4. Institutionalisation of cultural knowledge: The knowledge developed regarding culture and cultural dynamics, must be integrated into every facet of a service.
5. Adapt to diversity: Cultural practices should be adapted to develop new tools for substance misuse treatment.

Cultural competence is not a means to an end or an exact science. It is rooted in the notions of history, social inequality, and marginalization of section of the community. It is only as strong as the commitment to implement such a vision for change. The deployment of creative approaches that are adaptable across cultural boundaries ensure that cultural competence is embedded within the overall dissemination strategy, both methodologically and creatively. To do so I further call for researchers operating in a community context to embrace 'strength-based approaches' combined with 'action learning' when formulating dissemination strategies designed to maximize on impact when sharing with communities who feel vulnerable about the way research is disseminated.

Strengths based approach

'Strengths based approaches' are required to enable individuals to take control and direct their own lives, learning, and aspirations in ways that are meaningful and productive to them. A strength-based approach offers the possibility of seeing opportunities, hope, and solutions rather than just problems and hopelessness. A strength-based approach further sees individuals as initiators and directors of the change process. This means working with and facilitating rather than fixing and dictating. Embracing a strength-based approach encourages seeing beyond the limitations so often imposed on individuals who are directed by so-called 'experts' and focuses attention on the potential of what can be. Two core principles that underpin a 'strengths-based approach' are:

- An absolute belief that every person has potential and it is their unique strengths and capabilities that will determine their evolving story as well as define who they are, not their limitations.
- Belief that change is inevitable and all individuals can succeed and improve themselves.

This position moves beyond the traditional 'deficit model' where an individual takes charge of charting their own pathway toward change, leadership, and future success. As 'data verbalization' is performed and rooted within a storytelling tradition it gives community members an interactive and sensory experience rooted in seeing, hearing, and interacting. In doing so, the receiver of the disseminated research may pass comment, share their ideas, or merely respond using their own stories and performances indicative of 'call and response' approaches, where the poet calls out, and the audience responds. If the expression of 'data verbalization' actualizes a collective response from those in attendance, other concerns may emerge that can also form the basis of community led 'action learning'.

Action learning

Action learning is a process that involves engaging with the collective knowledge and skills of small groups to 'reinterpret' and 'reframe' familiar patterns of thinking with a specific aim of producing 'fresh', 'new', and 'innovative ideas' (Revans, 1998). Data verbalization is an ideal conduit for action learning as it can enable individuals to grasp and engage with complex ideas in a simplified form. Action learning happens on three levels:

- ... about one's self;
- ... about the issue being tackled;
- ... about the process of learning itself.

Similarly, if the community are involved in adapting research themselves in collaboration with the researcher they are able to incorporate action learning principles such as:

- Learning gained by engaging and collaborating with others.
- Learning without action.
- Individuals are directly involved in their own learning.
- Individuals voluntarily choose a learning experience.
- The learning makes it more personally meaningful.

In running workshops and seminars on 'data verbalization' in community settings it is clearly evident that participants experience the stages of action learning which are:

- Having an experience.
- Reflecting on and analysing the experience.
- Concluding the experience.
- Applying the learning, planning the next steps.

Furthermore, 'data verbalization' has provided the impetus for participants to engage with the shared elements of action learning that transcends the workshop or seminar such as:

- Voluntarily joining the group activity (data verbalization).
- Regular meetings and agreed ways of working with research.
- Developing independent ideas that feed into the wider data verbalization process.

The resulting outcomes reveal significant benefits such as:

- Increased self-awareness and improved confidence.
- Ability to approach situations from a broader and more varied perspective.
- More proactive in problem solving and decision making.
- Increased capacity to giving and accepting feedback.
- Handling communication with more sensitivity and confidence.

Engagement

Action learning expressed through engaging with data verbalization can offer significant possibilities in the building and shaping awareness for communities involved in transformative activities. If there is a research gap between academia and community, dissemination must play a key role in cementing disconnected relationships. Moving research beyond the university requires delicate handling and sensitive implementation. Joined up working should not be the sole domain of the researcher or their institution. A conversation with an indigenous scholar at the Race Matters Symposium at the London School of Economics in 2018, Indigenous scholar Professor Chris Cuneen, informed me how Indigenous communities are no longer the repository of colonial ways of conducting research. He went on further to inform me how Indigenous communities have a rich history rooted in ancestral traditions that form the basis of how information is located, processed, and understood. It should, therefore, become critically important for researchers operating in contexts that have a strong spiritual connection to their cultures to be mindful of adhering to those concerns. With 'data verbalization' this process starts from the inception of the process. Inasmuch, once the research has been identified, the next phases establish the principles in which the work will operate and be received. Essentially, as data verbalization is performance driven, it is knowing who the audience is. Important here is that any terminology used to define impacts must be located within a context agreed with the hosts receiving the research. Sebba (2011) suggests a useful three-way distinction between:

- 'Knowledge transfer' and 'dissemination', terms which signify only 'the movement of evidence from one place to another in order to increase access, without directly attempting to simplify, interpret or translate findings'.
- 'Knowledge translation', 'knowledge mobilization', 'research brokerage', and 'research mediation', all of which may be taken to 'imply an intention to intervene in the process, for example, summarizing, interpreting, etc., so as to increase use'. But Sebba stresses that such terms 'do not of themselves, provide evidence of use'.
- 'Research use', 'research utilization' and 'implementation', which all 'imply evidence of direct influence on policy or practice'. This usage might seem to 'depend on stakeholders' retrospective perceptions'.

Sebba further expresses the view that the drivers for improving impacts, recording, and assessments, are at times weak, confined to external pressures from funders, strategic agencies, or policy makers. Sebba's position would suggest that the key drivers for impact are less democratic and require approaches that are driven more by 'need' not 'greed'. Other constraints are resistance coming from academic staff, to increased monitoring, scrutiny, or placing unrealistic expectations on the outcomes, which can result in a 'funding to fail' scenario. Therefore, any tangible outcomes must contest, challenge, and push against these restrictions. It is for this reason that I decided 'data verbalization' must be informed by academic principles ethically, but transcend the oppressive and biased assumptions that becomes part of the institutional control over much research. For disseminated research to have significant impact it must provide a template for the actualization of both theory and knowledge, to bring change and transformation of some sort.

For whose benefit is it?

With the advent of new assessment frameworks being applied to research institutions it is questionable for whose benefit these new set of rules are designed to benefit. When the yardstick for qualitative research is statistically measured, or ethnographic observations become the basis of devaluing the integrity of immersive approached to research, the battle lines are well and truly drawn between traditional scholars and scholar activists. There are just too many variables within research as a whole to standardize the criteria we judge research against. Rather than focus on leagues tables or how much money is brought into the institution there needs to be a greater acknowledgement within the governance of the so-called 'research industry' that research needs to be seen as a highly complex enterprise that requires a diverse range of methods, modes of analysis, dissemination strategies, etc., that needs to be considered and evaluated to bring satisfactory conclusions, change and ultimately transformative solutions that the research was designed to addressed. If there is space for research that tests a hypothesis that can reaffirm a government's claim acting as a social barometer, then research that highlights uncertainty, chaos, or fragmented realities should be recognition that not everything can be measured scientifically. It is my view that research that is deemed risky, controversial, or contentious must seek refuge outside of the academy. Or at best be accepted by the institution or funding agency that may be more appropriate to ensure the embedding of any outcomes are not subject to power laden vested interests.

Transcending the academy

Again, I would like to refer to my Indigenous friends. Finding a cure for poor health cannot be properly evaluated unless there is a critical assessment of the history that may have led to health decline in the first place. In the global north, we have an advanced industrial society where the production of knowledge is well resourced based on the economic generation of governments. If our institutions serve those governments, where do community members who differ ideologically gain access to the means of both production and distribution of their 'counter-narrative' recommendations? If those advanced industrial societies have the infrastructure to access, develop, and generate solutions to problems, how do marginalized groups access the drivers for change if they are excluded from the means of generating research? The processes by which researchers generate knowledge through discovery process, presented through theory and interpretation knowledge, can be problematic in the processes that are purely driven by institutions that are detached from the constituents they are supposed to serve. The inability to present new research into an existing body of knowledge can create results that can have adverse effects.

Dependency

In my own discipline of criminology, I have consumed so much work on stop and search, racialization within the prison service, and gangs, which has had little or no impact in communities, but the citing institution continues to access more resources, without assisting those same 'researched on' communities to provide its own solutions. Because joined-up scholarship and cross-disciplinary work tends to be undertaken by well-known authors and researchers, it may have disproportionately large effects in achieving influence, even though it remains fairly small in overall volume. When governments invest public money in higher education research, and even more so when businesses, foundations, or charities directly fund academic outputs, academics often see the difficulties in recording or demonstrating positive social outcomes as an inhibitor of future funding. Academic outputs can generate profiled citations and be evaluated for validity and reliability in numerous ways. But the 'where do we go from here?' or 'can we sustain this work?' questions can be left dormant as there is no commitment to sustainability. As researchers, we can get too caught up in applying for funding driven by commercial appetites where dubious claims are made without any robust and rigorous accountability to those the research serves, namely the community. This state of affairs not only devalues the research but destroys any credibility I may have with the communities I work in. We all need to make a living, but to what cost. For over four decades, I have served communities with integrity and have built trust along the way, which is the most invaluable resource at my disposal. I would go as far as saying that our ethics should also include additional considerations from the communities themselves. I know in my work with offenders that their perspectives on my craft is integral to the overall research design. To do so I have to ensure I developed a strong impact strategy.

Developing an impact strategy

When developing a dissemination strategy, it is important to scope out at what was done before. Similar to a literature review questions such as: What products were created previously? Which ones worked effectively? How did particular audiences respond? How did the outcomes enhance or impede the intended changes?

- **Is the timing right?** A timeline for disseminating research should be established. Equally as important is in predicting if the dissemination process may be hindered by audiences attending religious or spiritual festivals on your intended dissemination date. Furthermore, if the dissemination is to take place in closed institutions such as hospitals and prisons, what are the primary consideration to ensure the timing of the dissemination is appropriate as well as timely?

- **What are the resource implications?** Assessing budgetary implications is vital. Recognizing the effort that goes into successful dissemination, you need to be clear that you have used the right tools, struck the right balance among available tools, and received sufficient user feedback. With 'data verbalization' there are a range of measures that can be used, ranging from social media platforms, various digital apps, recorded responses captured on camera phones, etc. This approach can invaluable of planning future strategies as well as revealing important impact that can be posted directly on-line and shared with sponsors and funders. In doing more digitized approaches to capturing responses you could attract potential sponsors who are trying to connect to the same demographic. As a researcher you can then synthesize all of this information into a lessons learned or best-practice document, than can also be adapted into a 'data verbalization' story.
- **Which audience/s do you need to impact?** Determining the primary and secondary audiences for the information being disseminated is a critical aspect of the dissemination strategy. As a researcher, you should understand who your audience is, how they absorb research evidence, their timelines, needs, etc. This will greatly increase the likelihood that the dissemination approach will meet its objectives. One tested way to ensure your team addresses the needs of all stakeholders in the dissemination process is to classify them into primary and secondary audiences. Primary audiences are those who need to make a decision or a change. Secondary audiences are those in a position to influence the decisions or actions of the primary audience. The level of audience (primary or secondary) is determined by the dissemination objectives. No matter how good the dissemination strategy is, it will have very little impact if it is not shared in the right format according to the identified needs of the audience. Above any other consideration, the delivery mechanism for disseminating your research dictates who receives, and therefore who might act upon, messages contained within the research itself.
- **What do you hope to achieve?** Having clarity and grounding your expectation regarding the outcomes you're wanting to achieve is a vital part of ensuring the audience are the recipients of mutually agreed desires. Messages are at the heart of any dissemination strategy. Messages should be direct, simple, and explain the problem the research sets out to address. In addition, the solution the research may have generated, the particular implications of the research findings, and/or what might be expected of different audiences as a consequence of those findings should be captured in the message. Messages should reflect the audience's needs and abilities with respect to the research evidence.

Case examples

- Silenced
- Article 51
- 1000 Words
- Ode to Rosa

Since its inception, I have used the 'data verbalization method in a variety of situations and contexts to great effect. I refer to the outputs of adapting my research and that of others as 'data verbalization stories'. To date, I have had my work featured on all major social media platforms: YouTube, Twitter, Spotify, iTunes, LinkedIn, Deezer, Amazon, to name but a few. The following are out there and having significant impact:

- Silenced – focuses on the issue of race and crime. As stated previously, I had grown tired of the lack of real support for my work around critical race theory and crime with relation to the peer review system. I was also perturbed by the lack of response to some of my colleagues when it came to returning to their previous constituencies to give an update on any progress emerging out of the recommendations in their research. My desire to deconstruct and adapt my work for popular consumption is what was and still is at the core of data verbalization. The breakthrough and subsequent impact were not in the subject matter, but the mode of dissemination that created an entertaining, thought provoking, and immersive experience of research data. Although the original piece was initially adapted for a conference, its wider appeal has come from music artists across the world who are now considering using research as baseline material for their own work.
- Article 51 – was a response to the Brexit negotiations. I had written another paper on mass incarceration and discussed the impacts of insecure Government policies on crime and communities. Unable to get the article published or considered in peer review journals, I was approached by a journalist who promptly put the adapted version of my article into a audioboom.com – ow.ly/lcuq309qLxt. On release of the podcast it was reviewed in a black music magazine. https://preview.mailerlite.com/e1y3k5/574897919543477745/p2h6/. Again, the impact was significant as the podcast and review in the music magazine brought my adapted article to the attention of a global audience.
- 1000 Words – For over three decades I had been working on the issue of 'father absence' with a reasonable amount of success. Many papers, research, conferences followed. However, I never thought that the issue was taken seriously by politicians, so I shelved the work. In 2010, I undertook a Winston Churchill Fellowship in Baltimore (USA) where I investigated the impact of father absence on the city. On my return I wrote a report and was awarded the 'pol-roger' award for services to the community. Again, the work was shelved as the promotion of my findings was fleeting. After the success of my first data verbalization single 'silenced' I was approached by my good friend and producer of data verbalization Richard Campbell who gave me a piece of instrumental music and asked me if I had any lyrics I could put with it. After careful reflection I went back to my years of work on father absence, and 1000 Words was born. After the initial release on iTunes the impact was huge. So much so that we decided to put a video on YouTube. This put my years of work back on the international platform, alongside bringing my work to the attention of audiences ranging from prison, social services, and radio stations. It

was a watershed moment, as well as a timely reminder how democratic these mediums were in giving a platform to hidden stories.

- Ode to Rosa – It is an adaptation of US academic Shadd Maruna's article, Desistance as a Social Movement featured in the Irish Probation Journal Volume (14), October 2017. Both myself and Richard recognized in the development phase of 'data verbalization' that the real test of its possibilities would be in the adaptation of other researchers work. I was a huge support of Shadd's work, as he was a leading criminology scholar who had always supported me throughout my career on both the personal and professional front. It was during a trawling through some recent developments in the desistance literature I came across Shadd's article. Not only did it resonate with me, but I was curious as to how impacting the article itself was. In communicating with Shadd, I shared my vision for extending the reach of 'data verbalization' and inquired is he would like me to put his article out onto the streets. At first, he was hesitant and slightly dubious. After several emails that required me to reassure him that the integrity of his work wouldn't be harmed, he finally agreed.

You can listen and see these data verbalization tracks on YouTube, iTunes, Amazon, Deezer, and Spotify, and view it on YouTube.

Conclusion

In 2018, I was featured in the *Sunday Times* Alternative Rich List, as an emerging thought leader. Central to the article was the creation of 'data verbalization'. The importance here was my new method had now breached the walls of academia and planted itself firmly in the global readership of this influential list. As we lived in a messy, complex, and at times toxic world, the impact of research for social justice goals becomes even more important and necessary for marginalized communities. These impacts take place in many settings. A journal article may improve business or governmental processes, but it may also help to make poor decisions also. With the increase pressure placed on researchers to bring money in to the university how do we ensure that research outputs do not always pander to the systems of academic profit and loss? We must strive always to develop much better ways of sharing knowledge when it comes to the primary impacts of research externally. Generating better ways to disseminate research as outlined in this chapter requires researchers to not only think outside the box, but to be prepared to sacrifice some of the fringe benefits associated with our craft. Guetzkow (2002) sees research impact as a burgeoning and wide-ranging field of research. Despite the variety of research subjects and methodologies alive and well in the field, there are a number of avenues this literature has yet to explore, data verbalization being one such approach. Bulaitis (2017) similarly argues that while there is a wealth of social science research that explores evaluation methods and assessment culture there is a lack of research into performance-driven dissemination techniques associated with generating impact. Bulaitis also expresses the view that policymakers should now pay attention to alternative values that require progressive researchers to address new debates and discourses regarding research impact. Again, data verbalization offers both a challenge and opportunity to expand any contemporary dialogue concerning research and its wider impacts. Denzin and Giardina (2017) have a perspective where researchers are seen as uniquely equipped to take up the challenge, to reach beyond the walls of the profession, to engage with disparate and competing publics, to conduct research that materially effects if not changes the course of historical presence. It is my view that 'data verbalization' is part of a historical continuum reflected in music such as: blues, jazz, reggae, hip-hop, and lately, grime. The central tenet for each one of the aforementioned genres was 'how the voice of oppressed people could be heard as a call to arms for social change and transformation'. It is my contention that if research can be presented through music, data verbalization can operate in the same way, where the researcher becomes the community storyteller, using research data, operating much the same as the lyrical forms previously mentioned.

Summary

This position chapter focused on the contentious issue of data driven 'reach' versus 'impact'. Similar to 'data visualization', that presents data in visual formats to explore difficult concepts or identify emerging new patterns contained within 'statistical data', it is my contention that 'data verbalization' can fulfil a complimentary function for qualitative researchers, wanting to disseminate data using performative means.

Reflective questions

- How do you assess the current framing of how research impact is measured?
- How do you reconcile the conflict between compliance within the academy and the social justice needs of the wider community in relation to your research dissemination strategies?

References

Arts Council (2006) *Visual Arts: Evidence of Impact*, London: Arts Council of England.
Barak, G., Flavin, J. & Leighton, P.S. (2001) *Class, Race, Gender, and Crime: Social Realities of Justice in America*, Los Angeles, CA: Roxbury.
Beckett, M. (2000) *Modernising Government in Action: Realising the Benefits of Y2K*, London: HMSO.
Bell, D. (1995) *Critical Race Theory: The Key Writings that Formed the Movement*, New York: The New Press.
Brown, K. (2005) 'Introducing research methods and self - authorship into undergraduate corporate communications curriculum', *Journal of the Pennsylvania Communication Association*.

Burgess-Proctor, A (2006) 'Intersections of race, class, gender, and crime', *Feminist Criminology*, 1(1): 27–47.

Bulaitis, Z. (2017) *Measuring Impact in the Humanities: Learning from Accountability and Economics in a Contemporary History of Cultural Value*, London: Palgrave.

Choo, H.Y. & Ferree, M.M. (2010) 'Practicing intersectionality in sociological research: A critical analysis of inclusions, interactions, and institutions in the study of inequalities', *Sociological Theory*, 28(2): 130–149.

Covington, J. (1995) 'Racial classification in criminology: The reproduction of racialised crime', *Sociological Forum*, 10(4): 547–568.

Denzin, N.K. (2010) *The Qualitative Manifesto*, Walnut Creek, CA: Left Coast Press.

Denzin, N.K. & Giardana, M. (2017) *Qualitative Inquiry in Neo Liberal Times*, New York: Routledge.

Freire, P. (1970) *Pedagogy of the Oppressed*, London: Continuum.

Glynn, M. (2014) *Black Men, Invisibility, and Crime: Towards a Critical Race Theory of Desistance*, London: Routledge.

Guetzkow, J. (2002) *How the Arts Impact Communities: An Introduction to the Literature on Arts Impact Studies*, Princeton, NJ: Princeton.

Lipsky, M. (1980) *Street-level Bureaucracy: Dilemmas of the Individual in Public Services*, New York: Russell Sage Foundation.

Revans, R. (1998) *ABC of Action Learning* (3rd edn), London: Lemos and Crane.

Sebba, J. (2011) How do research mediators enhance or inhibit social science knowledge transfer? Paper to the Knowledge Transfer Seminar Series. London School of Economics.

6

DATA VERBALIZATION AND THE PRESENTATION OF SELF

This chapter calls for the embodied elements of the researcher's reflexive and autoethnographic accounts to become both 'audible' and 'visible' through the expression of a 'performed story'. In my own reflexive position as a non-white, critical race theorist, criminologist from an inner-city background, I embody multiple identities. At times when I have experienced self-doubt, emotional upset, or distress, I explore and examine the consequences and impacts of my choices upon the research process via poetry, song, theatre, and lately 'data verbalization'. This performance-driven intersection highlights how my work as a researcher at times experiences clear bias and subjectivity. This approach further highlights how the inner decisions I made throughout the research journey itself impacted on my outer workings as a researcher. It is therefore my view that any personal baggage, and at times, flawed assumptions made should, if appropriate, be shared publicly. In doing so I move my private research experience/s contained within my diary, into a public shared space bringing much-needed sharing with those I've co-produced with. By immersing myself in the world of my own story and sharing it, I am making myself accountable to those I have engaged with along the way. Again, this is not a call for researchers to follow this approach, but it reaffirms my own commitment regarding ethical choices made during the research. Reflexivity and autoethnography therefore become an act of self-referral designed to generate some level of accountability between the researcher and the subjects of the inquiry. I will further present case examples of this approach when using 'data verbalization'. I am also keen to stress that this element of **positionality** extends beyond the incorporation into our methodological choices.

Researcher's metaphor

When an individual breaks the law they are arrested, face a (performed) trial in front of an audience (jury), where characters (witnesses) are called into a staged scene (court-room) to present both sides of the accused life and behaviours (backstory). The resulting outcome is either freedom, or loss of liberty, if found guilty. Goffman's 1959 notion of 'the presentation of self' similarly acts as a 'researcher's metaphor' when presenting embodied experiences through performance. Goffman explored how theatrical perfor-mance may be applied to personal interactions and posited that individuals 'change' or 'fix' their appearance/s and manner/s when they come in contact with others in an attempt to control or guide the impression that others might make of them. I contend that by occupying racialized 'white spaces' I am called upon to perform notions of my blackness that at times become entangled in the site where my research is being con-ducted. In doing so I have to construct insights and understandings where the intersec-tional 'mask' I wear is removed and further interrogated (Turner, 1969). My embodied racialized persona therefore is presented through reflexivity, auto-ethnographic accounts, and performed in a space that reveals those interactions.

Dunbar (1892) explores this notion of 'ontological reflection' where he writes:

> we wear the mask that grins and lies;
> it hides our cheeks and shades our eyes,
> this debt we pay to human guile;
> with torn and bleeding hearts we smile.
> *(Dunbar, 1892: 167)*

Dunbar's verse highlights a deep psychic challenge for researchers such as myself as the 'wear(ing)' of the racialized mask undermines positive constructs of myself, that in turn restricts me becoming 'the author of my own life' (McAdams, 1988). Dunbar's image of 'torn and bleeding hearts' further suggests that, in spite of the pain and burden of an oppressive history of slavery, colonialism, and racism, I am forced to put on a brave face, and don a 'mask' in order to survive black oppression and subsequent subordination in predominant white spaces. The need for me to reveal my 'own truths' therefore becomes significant if I am to transcend my 'racial subordination' within academia and the wider research community. DeFranz and Gonzalez (2014) argue that the embodiment of black performance socially emerges as a consideration about how we begin to name the mechanism/s of black pre-sence, alongside presenting a counter narrative that can decentralize oppressive research paradigms. Denzin (2018) offers a supportive voice to the dilemma of critical researchers by seeing performance based human disciplines as contributing to social change and cultural politics. As Chang (2008) reminds me that if auto-ethnography is about self-narrative it should transcend mere narration of 'self' to engage with cultural analysis and personal interpretation. This in my view not only legitimizes performing my research blackness as a political act, but it is a position that white academics must engage with as a way of accounting reflexively for their whiteness. I similarly argues that when staged performance becomes an element in the representation of research data, into physical performance is a powerful and translation from the page to the stage. The validity of the words spoken or physicalized, has the power to evoke emotional responses from the observer (audience). Mienczakowski further highlights how reflexivity constructed through performance is a powerful tool for gaining insight, understandings, and the perceived depiction of the lived realities of researcher. I refer to this position as 'breaking the fourth wall'.

Breaking the fourth wall

Throughout this section I will draw on some of my experiences which required me to 'talk to self' and share 'self' with others. I come to this position having spent over three decades 'performing' self on a variety of platforms and contexts; lecturing, workshop facilitation, poetry, theatre, stand up-comedy, and lately TEDx. The (re)presentation of my 'self' using performance uses the theatrical tradition of 'breaking the fourth wall'. The term fourth wall applies to the imaginary invisible wall at the front of the stage in a theatre through which the audience sees the action in the world of the play. The term signifies the suspension of disbelief by the audience, who are looking in on the action through the invisible wall. The audience thus pretends that the characters in the story are 'real living' beings in their own world, and not merely actors performing on a stage or studio set, or written words on the pages of a book. In order for the fourth wall to remain intact, the actors must also, in effect, pretend that the audience does not exist, by staying in character at all times and by not addressing the audience members directly. When I speak my data directly to an audience, I embody myself through the intersection of the physical, emotional, oral, political, and cultural. In doing so I reveal myself. In my junior days as a researcher it was not uncommon for me to write reflexively from a standpoint of revealing my inner thoughts, biases, and other related experiences purely on paper. By extending my researcher vernacular using a creative process such as 'data verbalization' to inform the presentation of (my) self, I locate those experiences within an open and vulnerable space, open to gaze and scrutiny. Performing reflexively therefore is about finding strategies to question not just my attitudes, thought processes, values, assumptions, prejudices and habitual actions, but it moves (my)self beyond someone who merely undertakes reflection as practical exercise with little or no accountability.

Reflexivity and me

It is my view that 'performing reflexively' can assist the researcher, research participants, and communities outside of the academy in understanding the challenges faced by the researcher when conducting the research. This critical focus upon beliefs, values, professional identities, and how they affect, and are affected, by the surrounding cultural structures, is an overt social and political act. It should enhance the role of the researcher as a 'trusted other' by building confidence with the researcher's constituency. In essence, performance reflexivity becomes an integral, not a separate element of the research enquiry itself. Mauthner and Doucet (2003) argue for the importance of being reflexive is acknowledged within social science research, the difficulties, practicalities, and methods of doing it are rarely addressed. Thus, the implications of current theoretical and philosophical discussions about reflexivity, epistemology, and the construction of knowledge for empirical sociological research practice, specifically the analysis of qualitative data, remain underdeveloped. Mauthner and Doucet further argue that data analysis methods are not mere neutral techniques, but are imbued with, theoretical, epistemological and ontological assumptions – including conceptions of subjects and subjectivities, and understandings of how knowledge is constructed and produced.

Incorporation

Mauthner and Doucet suggest that epistemological and ontological positionings should be incorporated through our research practice as part of the nitty-gritty of research practice. I too share their concerns by arguing that abstract themes if the visible context is absent does not make the research journey fully rounded. Emirbayer and Desmond (2012) recognize that our understanding of the sociological order will remain unsatisfactory if we fail to turn our analytic gaze back upon ourselves and inquire critically into the hidden presuppositions that shape our thought. However, for reflexivity to be employed widely in the interest of pursuit of a series of truths, researchers must acknowledge reflexive thinking as much more than observing how our respective social positioning affects and impacts on the process of analysis. Mills (1959) sees the challenge before us is to develop a methodology that allows us to examine how the private troubles of individuals are connected to public issues and to pubic responses to those troubles. Similarly, Denzin and Giardina (2017) express the view that qualitative researchers of all traditions are ideally equipped to reach beyond the wall of the academy, to engage competing publics, and to conduct research that changes the course of historical presence. Denzin (2010) further expresses the view that each generation must articulate its epistemological, methodological, and ethical stance toward critical inquiry. It is here I would like to turn my attention to indigenous ways of knowing. Within the scientific methods the absence of a spiritual role within research further exacerbates the hegemonic assumptions that at times becomes the bedrock of western forms of knowledge production.

Indigenous ways of seeing

Brown and Strega (2005) assert that Indigenous ways of knowing are inextricably linked to Indigenous ways of doing by honouring the oral tradition of the ancestors expressed through storytelling. Ellingsworth (2017) presents a view that all research depends on the participant's participation but participatory approaches that share power and control with participants. Sharing power and control enables bodies to move freely, less constrained by the embodied power of researcher academic credentials and emphasises the value of participants' perspectives and knowledge that is grounded in their daily lives. Therefore, Indigenous researchers confront scientific researchers who ignore or render ancestral input into the research process null and void. How does the co-creation of meanings describe how a person comes to understand reality? Namely, what if those complex meanings of describing reality is rooted in ancient traditions? The Self as Mead (1932) argues that it is socially constructed in our everyday social encounters with others and is reflexively involved in its experiences. Alvesson and Skoldberg (2009) feel that serious attention paid to the different kinds of linguistic, social, political, and theoretical elements are woven together in the process of knowledge development, during which empirical material is constructed, interested, and written. Carstensen-Egwuom (2013) sees embodied reflexive practice requiring critical concepts like intersectionality to shed light on theoretical 'blind spots' concerning the politics of fieldwork and the way academic knowledge production is embedded in struggles for symbolic power. Ultimately it is the researcher as storyteller who must take the ingredients of the research story, mould them, and share them in a unique and authentic way. To illustrate this, I would like to share some of my own reflexive account during my doctoral study.

Using data verbalization to perform reflexively

This reflexive part of my doctoral research focuses on how my own racial identity impacted on my ability to remain objective throughout the research journey. It also acted as an analytical tool to assess if my 'insider' position in the research would hinder my objectification throughout the research journey. Total impartiality was impossible, as operating as 'the insider' gave me a unique insight into the world of the subjects of the inquiry where there were obvious risks involved. My reflexivity revealed how relinquished some level of control within the research process, as a way of enabling the voices of my participants to be heard. For as Duneier (2006) argues, participants in research should become owners of their stories and in doing so experience dignity within the research process. This is a view echoed by Becker who states, 'We focus too much on questions whose answers show that the supposed deviant is morally in the right and the ordinary citizen morally in the wrong' (Becker, 1967: 240). It was therefore wholly appropriate for black men in my study who have been rendered invisible in many research studies not only to be given voice to share their understanding and insights, but to further give an offender/reformed offender perspective. Therefore, the reflexive aspect of the research was designed to identify the ongoing conflict between the objective and subjective aspects of the research itself. Frequently the view expressed by my co-producer was that occupying a 'safe space' where they don't have to defend their cultural perspectives; linguistic codes or expressions of blackness, became a liberating factor within the research process. My research started from an interpretivist perspective. That is, the research focused on the meanings that black men give to their lived experiences of fatherhood, re-entry, and desistance (McAdams, 1985). It further sought to enable black men to explore and narrate their own story in dramatic form and aimed to encourage them to find an outlet for self-examination using creative expression as the conduit. Denzin (2010) suggests that 'at the beginning of a new century it is necessary to re-engage the promise of qualitative research as a form of radical democratic process. We know the world only through our representations of it (2010: 6). As a consequence of the difficulties I faced conducting my doctoral research overall, I struggled to accept the disproportionate way I felt I was treated by my colleagues and wanted to find an outlet for critical examination that would lead to some much-needed healing. So, I adapted my reflexive diary into a piece of ethnodrama called 'White Space'.

Synopsis

'White Space' is a tense one act ethnodrama featuring the complexities, contradictions, and tensions surrounding the occupation of 'white space' by Dr Tyrone Valentine, a lecturer in a predominantly white university. The play examines the binary of 'assimilation' versus 'integration', when a Tyrone's 'pro-black' stance comes into conflict when he accuses the Dean of the university as operating through a 'colour blind' lens. With a continuing sense of frustration of feeling marginalized within the academy criminology lecturer Dr Tyrone Valentine publicly speaks out against his university for taking an apolitical stance on all things 'race' and creates a 'students forum' aimed at contesting the universities 'colour blind' mindset. During a heated debate in a lecture a near fight breaks out between some of Tyrone's students and some right-wing students. The incident makes its way into the newspapers where the university is branded 'institutionally racist' bringing out a storm of protest from the surrounding black community. The resulting outcome creates increased tension among some of the students who have set up a 'black student's society' within the university itself. Fearful of the impact that this situation may have on the university and its reputation, the Dean of the University Professor Joseph Dawkins summons Dr Valentine to a meeting to discuss the student's actions. In a heated exchange Dr Valentine is told that he must cease his connection to the students and the 'black student's society', warning him that there will be significant consequences. Unable to contain his anger Dr Valentine unpacks his experiences at being a black academic within a white space. The rising tension pushes Professor Dawkins to accuse Dr Valentine of being contentious, controversial, and not acting in the best interests of the university. As their heated discussion grows, a deep rift threatens to destroy both of their careers. As Professor Dawkins struggles to uphold his white privileged position, Dr Valentine similarly struggles to preserve his sense of 'blackness' as a consequence of feeling oppressed within the 'white space'. The news of another shooting by the police of an unarmed young black man in the US punches through the moment, forcing both Professor Dawkins and Dr Valentine to pause for reflection. This tipping point moment has a profound impact on both men who have to confront some powerful truths about 'race' within the wider society. White space addresses the existential issues of 'white privilege' in academia, while at the same time exploring how black activist scholars struggle to navigate the 'white space' as a condition of their 'racial existence'.

Characters

Professor Joseph Dawkins – White, middle aged, Dean of the University.
Dr Tyrone Valentine – Black, middle aged, senior lecturer in criminology.

Scene one – The confrontation

Dean of the University, **Professor Joseph Dawkins**, *a middle-aged white man sits in his office, holding a bunch of papers. He looks vacantly just above its wilting page and occasionally stares blankly toward the window.* **Dr Tyrone Valentine** *enters and lowers himself onto the chair opposite Professor Dawkins, searches through his bag and removes a series of papers, which he places on the edge of the desk. Tyrone's defiant posture unnerves Professor Dawkins who coughs nervously.*

JOSEPH: Tyrone.
TYRONE: (Coldly) Professor Dawkins.
JOSEPH: Come on. Let's drop the formality. It's Craig.

> (*Tyrone nods his head. Professor Dawkins is visibly uncomfortable and nervously shuffles papers on his desk before regaining his composure. The two men stare at each other like two chess opponents.*)

JOSEPH: I presume you know why you're here?
TYRONE: Vaguely
JOSEPH: Vaguely?
TYRONE: *(Guarded)* As I said, *vaguely.*
JOSEPH: So why do you think I asked you to come and see me?
TYRONE: You called this meeting. You tell me. *(Takes out a note pad from his bag and slams it on the table.)*
JOSEPH: *(Nervously)* Look Tyrone, I don't want this meeting to get off to a rocky start. I just want to sort this mess out. Do you understand?
TYRONE: *(Terse)* … and I don't want this meeting to be conducted where you lecture me as if I'm a student. Do *you* understand?

> (*Professor Dawkins stares hard at Tyrone but looks away as the stare is reciprocated. Professor Dawkins catches a glimpse of the note pad and shuffles nervously on his seat.*)

JOSEPH: *(Glares)* Why the note pad?
TYRONE: Do you have a problem with it?

(*Professor Dawkins struggles to conceal his upset, as Tyrone pulls out a micro recorder and positions it strategically on the desk.*)

Would you prefer I use this instead?

JOSEPH: Is there a need for this?
TYRONE: I don't want to be misquoted.

(*Like a chess player with the winning move, Tyrone falls back into his chair with an air of smugness about him. Professor Dawkins body language becomes awkward, combined with more nervous shuffling on his chair.*)

JOSEPH: This meeting is informal.
TYRONE: (Puts the cassette player back into his bag) I'm still going to take notes.
JOSEPH: (Terse) I'll get straight to the point then.

(*Tyrone takes up an offensive posture.*)

During one of your recent lectures, a near fight broke out between some of your students. Is that true?

TYRONE: If that's what you want to call it.
JOSEPH: It was either a fight or it wasn't?
TYRONE: There was a heated debate based on the differences of opinion being expressed in the lecture. The class was divided on their views. That's normal in my class. It was tense at times, but nothing I couldn't control. The students tend to respect the way I encourage debates around subjects that are controversial. The subject brought out a lot of strong emotion in everyone. I thought it was appropriate to create a space for them to talk about it.
JOSEPH: So, what led to the fight?
TYRONE: After the lesson had finished, some of the students carried on arguing throughout their break and it spilled over into the library.
JOSEPH: Didn't you try to stop it?
TYRONE: I wasn't around. It was during their own break. I have no jurisdiction there.
JOSEPH: But you must have thought something was going to happen?
TYRONE: Why? Arguments take place all the time. It's the nature of the subject.
JOSEPH: But from what I heard, you incited the conflict.
TYRONE: I didn't incite anything.
JOSEPH: Your personal views have no place being aired in the classroom. Especially around sensitive issues. Your classroom should be a space for you to direct students learning, not a platform for your own 'radical' views.
TYRONE: Radical views?
JOSEPH: If we all allowed our own politicised views to creep into every lecture, then where would we be? I myself have strong views on many things, but it

would be inappropriate for me to express them in public, let alone a classroom full of impressionable minds

TYRONE: *(Attacking)* I'm a criminologist. How can I avoid subjectivity in the classroom? Are you suggesting that the people we teach are that naive that they don't have an opinion on the issues of the day? You of all people should know that, you used to teach politics and philosophy.

JOSEPH: When I used to teach I always steered the class towards the content of the curriculum. And if a debate took place, it was in context. My own views were never put forward. For me it's about creating an environment where you enable the students to learn with your guidance, not direct influence.

TYRONE: So, you want my classroom to become a sterile place where my students just soak in what we tell them without question?

(Long and uncomfortable silence)

I don't have to justify my actions. Judge me by my results. I've never had any complaints.

JOSEPH: We've never had an incident like this before.

TYRONE: Maybe the university should see this moment as a way of listening to the concerns of students before it gets to this point?

JOSEPH: The fact remains, the consequences of this incident means that the press are now all over us? And that's not good.

TYRONE: Not good for who? What's your point?

JOSEPH: My point is that this adverse publicity will have a marked effect on public relations of the university. We can't afford stuff like this getting out at a time when we're trying to attract the best students to come here.

TYRONE: I still don't see what this has got to do with me.

JOSEPH: Come on Tyrone. Let's not play the innocent here.

TYRONE: I'm not playing the innocent? There was a fight on campus! My students were involved! I'm sure the university has adequate procedures to deal with such matters. Some of the students went to the press, and you want to blame me?

JOSEPH: I'm not blaming you, but it was your students that cried racism to the press was it not?

TYRONE: Hold on a minute. They may have been my students, but they did what they did off their own back. It had nothing to do with me.

JOSEPH: Indirectly it was.

TYRONE: In what way?

(Professor Dawkins composes himself and takes a deep breath.)

JOSEPH: Some of your colleagues have told me you have a radical teaching style that favours the black students.

TYRONE: Favours the black students?

JOSEPH: I've also had feedback from some of the white students, who say the same thing.

TYRONE: So, this is a witch hunt then? You've been investigating me.

JOSEPH: No! I'm merely responding to some of the concerns that have been expressed by colleagues and some students, as a consequence of what took place.

TYRONE: Why didn't those students come and see me?

JOSEPH: Some of the students who weren't involved have been quite impacted and reported it to some of your colleagues as they were frightened to raise it with you directly.

TYRONE: So why didn't my colleagues come and talk to me face to face?

JOSEPH: I don't know. You should take it up with them. That's not my concern right now. I'm merely trying to point out how you are seen by some of the students, who see your stance on things as not all inclusive.

TYRONE: Do I take a position as a black man in my class? Absolutely! Do I expect my students to take a position in the class? Absolutely!

JOSEPH: Isn't that a bit irresponsible on your part?

TYRONE: Irresponsible? When have other members of the teaching staff at this university ever apologized for their views?

(*Another awkward silence*)

Students relate to me and feel safe to express their concerns. Surely, that's what all lecturers are supposed to do?

JOSEPH: So you don't feel in anyway responsible for what took place?

TYRONE: (*Shakes his head*) No!

JOSEPH: Is it true that you held a recent seminar advocating that we should have a Black Lives Matter campaign here on campus?

TYRONE: You're inaccurate, it was the black student's society who invited me to attend one of their monthly debates. There's nothing wrong with that.

JOSEPH: Do you think we need a Black Lives Matter campaign here in the university?

TYRONE: What kind of question that?

JOSEPH: It's relevant to this issue. If you are advocating for Black Lives Matter, it clearly demonstrates that you weren't objective about what took place in your classroom.

(*Tyrone gets agitated, jumps to his feet, and faces off at Professor Dawkins, who pushes his chair back, gets to his feet, and paces nervously*)

TYRONE: Why are you doing that?

JOSEPH: You're displaying aggression?

TYRONE: Aggression! Are you mad? I'm upset at the way you're talking to me, that's all.

(Professor Dawkins returns to his seat and regains his composure. Tyrone sits down. There is an uncomfortable silence)

You wanna know what I think about Black Lives Matter? They're no different to any group who feels squeezed or marginalized on campus.

JOSEPH: So, you agree with them then?

TYRONE: In principle.

JOSEPH: In principle?

TYRONE: They have legitimate concerns.

JOSEPH: How so? Black Lives Matter is not a university Issue.

TYRONE: Police brutality on young Black men isn't an issue?

JOSEPH: *(Blankly)* I can't see its relevance here.

TYRONE: Over the past few weeks I listened to students talk about everything from Syria to Brexit, have you outlawed that?

JOSEPH: Setting up an organized response to issues beyond the universities control is different.

TYRONE: No, it isn't. Our students should be involved in debates, it's part of developing their curiosity.

JOSEPH: Not if it involves violence

TYRONE: For weeks, I've had students approaching me and asking me why there isn't enough black content in the courses here. Hence, they put on a seminar to gauge what the mood was from other students. With recent events in the media they felt they would get a better response if they organized themselves under the banner of Black Lives Matter, and it obviously worked. You know the paradox of this situation, there were quite a few white students echoing the same thing ...

JOSEPH: *(Interrupts)*... I'm confused. Why should they be talking about Black Lives Matter specifically? This is a university.

TYRONE: *(Interrupts)*. maybe because they're tired and fed up of having to learn about theories and ideas that lack any real diversity. Maybe they're looking at where do Black Lives Matter in the academy, in the curriculum, in the staffing ...

JOSEPH: *(Snaps and cuts him off)* ... this is Birmingham, not Chicago or Atlanta.

TYRONE: *(Snaps back)* When was the last time you walked around the university?

JOSEPH: What do mean?

TYRONE: Nearly half the students here are non-white, yet the curriculum, staff, and library resources are still exclusively white.

JOSEPH: *(Defensive)* What has that got to do with the allegation of institutional racism in the press? You're straying off the point. We've gone from an incident in the classroom to talking about Black Lives Matter.

TYRONE: This is all connected?

JOSEPH: Connected? Where?

TYRONE: Do you honestly believe that the students you've got here are going to accept subjects and staff that are pure white without question. We're in 2016, not 1916.

There is little reflection of the diversity of the student's backgrounds in any aspect of the way this university does its business. Surely our students should expect more of a university that prides itself on offering a wide and varied curriculum?

JOSEPH: Don't place the race card.

TYRONE: And you don't play the White Privilege card either.

JOSEPH: *(Defensive)* Listening to you right now I can see how you've probably instigated this whole affair.

TYRONE: *(Attacking)* Why are you avoiding the issue?

JOSEPH: *(Defensive)* I'm not

TYRONE: Yes, you are.

JOSEPH: There's far more pressing matters to deal with right now. That's why I wanted you to come and account for yourself.

TYRONE: I'm not on trial here.

JOSEPH: But it *was* your students who created the problem.

TYRONE: They're not my students. They are students of *this* university who felt compelled to report this university to the press as they were fed up of not having their voices heard. And more importantly many of them are tired of the way they are being talked down to every time they ask questions or challenge members. So, they decided to organize themselves.

JOSEPH: Why did they feel the need to go to the press? They could have resolved it internally.

TYRONE: Simple.

JOSEPH: Simple?

TYRONE: After the fight broke out some of the students approached the black students' society, who then approached several members of the faculty.

JOSEPH: What happened?

TYRONE: Nothing. That's what happened.

JOSEPH: I'm not clear.

TYRONE: Attempts to organise the event were thwarted by several members of the faculty who felt it might create more tension.

JOSEPH: *(Sarcastic)* And of course you endorsed the students view?

TYRONE: I told them to seek permission through the right channels, although I was personally behind them.

JOSEPH: I feel the staff behaved appropriately.

TYRONE: That's not the issue here.

JOSEPH: What is the issue then?

TYRONE: Some students felt that the university was hypocritical in the way is dismissed their concerns.

JOSEPH: By students, you mean black students?

TYRONE: What do you mean black students?

JOSEPH: Well it was mostly black students who instigated the press complaint?

TYRONE: Let's get this straight. The black students were subjected to racist abuse from some of the white students. They've repeatedly made complaints, but have been ignored. It's not just black students that get upset. We have some really racist students, who sound more like Donald Trump than Barack Obama. The black students asserted themselves and used the proper channels. But when they got blocked they resorted to other means.

JOSEPH: *(Interrupts)* So you did know about it then?

(Tyrone remains quiet)

So why didn't you report it to the head of your department, so we could have nipped it in the bud?TYRONE: Nipped what in the bud? The students had a legitimate reason to raise some concerns and exercised their rights to do so. I've done nothing wrong. I don't have to listen to this. *(Goes to exit)*

JOSEPH: *(Calls out)* Go on. Walk away! You think it's that simple don't you? ...

(Tyrone turns abruptly, and lunges at Professor Dawkins. He composes himself and let's go of Professor Dawkins.)

TYRONE: *(Angry)* I'm not going to stand here and be talked down to by you.

JOSEPH: You think violence will solve the issue?

TYRONE: And you think sitting on the fence with your neo liberal attitude will change anything?

JOSEPH: Neo liberal attitude?

TYRONE: You heard me.

JOSEPH: You can't judge me

TYRONE: So, what are you then?

JOSEPH: *(Defensive)* You have no idea what I have to go through. You're not the only one affected by this situation.

TYRONE: And how are you affected by this?

JOSEPH: *(Dismissive)* Can we just move on?

(Tyrone lets out a sigh, looks in the air, and returns to the chair. His posture suggests he is ready to flip out at any moment.)

Surely there are channels that students can use if there's stuff they're not happy with? What about the students' union?

TRYONE: The student's union has no interest in real issues that affects the student's lives. They have no real power. The incident that took place was not a student's union issue.

JOSEPH: Why not?

TYRONE: It's beyond their remit.

JOSEPH: How do you know this?

TYRONE: *(Laughs to himself)* I've been here for well over a decade. That's how I know.

JOSEPH: Do you find this funny?

TYRONE: Not funny, Ironic.

JOSEPH: Ironic?

TYRONE: Check it. Why do you think black students don't like reporting stuff to the union?

JOSEPH: I don't have a clue.

TYRONE: As a senior lecturer I struggle to assert any sense of my blackness. What message do you think that sends out to students?

JOSEPH: That's not true. All you have to do is voice your concerns. If you choose to keep quiet, then it's no-one's fault.

TYRONE: Let's just get back to the issue?

JOSEPH: So why the press then?

TYRONE: The students had obviously had enough.

JOSEPH: I'm going to ask you again. Did you put them up to it? Even if informally?

TYRONE: I didn't need to.

JOSEPH: Didn't need to?

TYRONE: With all due respects, as the Dean of this university you're massively out of touch with what's going on in this university. The issue for me is how you respond now.

JOSEPH: But the damage has already been done.

TYRONE: So, what are you going to do about it?

JOSEPH: I thought you'd be able to provide me with some answers, but based on this conversation I'm beginning to wonder if that's possible.

TYRONE: Oh, I get it. The only black lecturer in the university has to sort out a situation that it alone created. Give me a break.

JOSEPH: You have a responsibility here …

TYRONE: *(Interrupts)* … alongside the other 35 white members of the faculty.

JOSEPH: *They* weren't responsible for creating this mess.

TYRONE: *(Angry)* … and, nor was I?

JOSEPH: *(Presses)* Okay, even if I accept your point. The fact remains, we *still* have problem?

TYRONE: If *we* have a problem, why am I the only one in here? Where's the other accusers?

JOSEPH: Because I don't feel other members of staff need to be directly involved.

Tyrone shakes his head and bites his lip

As I've been saying repeatedly I thought you might be able to assist in this matter.

TYRONE: That's not how you put it across originally.

JOSEPH: Look Dr Valentine we're not getting anywhere. Maybe we should start with your experience here.

TYRONE: This ain't about me.

JOSEPH: I think it is.

TYRONE: What makes you say that?

JOSEPH: You seem to echo the view that this university has debilitated you in some way, much the same as the students. Maybe, If I have a greater insight to the way things are through the eyes of a lecturer such as yourself

TYRONE: *(Snaps)* ...what do you mean, a lecturer such as myself?

JOSEPH: .... black and politicized. That's what I mean.

TYRONE: There are wider issues at stake here.

JOSEPH: I agree. But I do think it's important to hear your views on some of the issues you've raised.

(Long pause. Tyrone looks undecided.)

TYRONE: *(Half hearted)* Okay.

JOSEPH: You've been here over ten years, so how do you feel about that?

TYRONE: If I'm being honest, a lot of the times I feel 'trapped', which is at times is draining and painful in equal measures. I also feel disconnected and dislocated from what's going on in the university. To the point where I just wander around like a nomad in the desert.

JOSEPH: It can't be that bad *(pause)* can it?

TYRONE: At this university I feel at times I've been rendered 'invisible'.

JOSEPH: Invisible?

TYRONE: Ralph Ellison in his book 'Invisible man' has a character that feels he's invisible in a society that refuses to see who he really is. He gets frustrated and attacks a white man in the process. His logic being if he's seen as invisible then you can't see when you're being attacked.

JOSEPH: Are you saying that you feel invisible here?

TYRONE: As Ellison's character says I possess a mind, am a man of substance, but this university refuses to see me. My sense of 'who I am' at times is swallowed up by 'identity politics' in this place.

JOSEPH: Identity politics?

TYRONE: My difference as an intelligent, culturally and politically aware black man is at times fraught with many tensions and contradictions. When I do attempt to assert any sense of my own 'authenticity' it falls on deaf ears.

JOSEPH: I'm still not clear.

TYRONE: Basically, I'm labelled as an 'outsider' regardless of how I am packaged. I may have a doctorate, but I live in the community and have little in common with my other colleagues.

JOSEPH: But you must have made some friends here?

TYRONE: Not really, I'm always having to fit myself into their world. They have no interest in my world, until there's a problem like now. If they have a problem with a black student, then they send them to me. Other than that, there's little in the way of any real connection.

JOSEPH: But have you tried?

TYRONE: It's a two-way process.

JOSEPH: I'm still not clear about this invisibility you talk of.

TYRONE: A good friend of mine recently referred to me as being confined to the subs bench on a sports team, in spite of training hard and being very skilled at the game.

JOSEPH: But surely you've participated in the life of the university on equal terms. I find it hard to believe that a member of this university feels this way. For someone whose been here over ten years, why is this an issue now?

TYRONE: It's always been an issue.

JOSEPH: Why haven't you raised it with anyone?

TYRONE: *(Shouts)* I'm the only black lecturer in a university where 50% of the students look like me. Doesn't that strike you as wrong?

JOSEPH: You're losing me.

TYRONE: *(Angry but soft in tone)* As confident as I may appear on the outside, there are times when my flair, individuality, and operating outside the box, scares some members of your team who have been playing the same formation and tactics for far too long. I then find myself back on the subs bench, and dropped from the team for nothing more than having a different point of view. The word 'fear' comes to mind.

JOSEPH: Fear? Now I'm really confused.

TYRONE: In academia, when white people are fearful of you, they retreat, recede, and ignore you, rendering you 'invisible'. When I refuse to be 'invisible', I am slapped down, forced to compromise my integrity, and become part of other people's 'vested interests'.

JOSEPH: *(Sarcastic)* ... you do have a strong black image.

TYRONE: ... and what's that supposed to mean?

JOSEPH: *(Defensive)* Come on, you know what I mean.

TYRONE: What! because I'm not an Uncle Tom,

JOSEPH: Uncle Tom?

TYRONE: Sell out. Black on the outside, white on the inside. You must have heard the term?

JOSEPH: No.

TYRONE: *(Exasperated and to himself)* This ain't going nowhere

JOSEPH: I don't see the relevance.

TYRONE: Listen! I'm not a revolutionary with a single focus hell bent of destroying others who do not agree with my views on life. I believe in equality first and foremost.

JOSEPH: But who's stopping you?

TYRONE: *(Sighs and clasps his head in frustration)* I'm tired of being defined by white people's expectations. I decided a long time ago not succumb to the will of others, who feel that 'assimilation' is good for the control of my soul.

JOSEPH: Are you trying to say that you're not accepted on your own terms here?

TYRONE: How many times do I have to say it, on numerous occasions I have experienced what I can only describe as an obsessive need of some of my colleagues to assimilate me into their vested interests with nothing more than a desire to exert some level of control on me and my thinking.

JOSEPH: Are you sure you're not exaggerating?

TYRONE: Give me some credit, I'm an intelligent man.

JOSEPH: But sometimes we can exaggerate what we see.

TYRONE: African American author James Baldwin when living in exile in France wrote, 'once you find yourself in another civilization you're forced to examine your own'. Baldwin reminds me that my current existence within this university at times feels like I'm in exile.

JOSEPH: But you're not in exile. As academics we have many challenges. You're no different than the rest of us?

TYRONE: I'm tired of wrestling with the challenges of being a black male academic in a predominantly white institution who want me to surrender my identity.

JOSEPH: You've got a PhD, you're a senior lecturer, and you continue to research your interests. So, I'm bemused how you feel you have to surrender your identity.

TYRONE: When my mannerisms, demeanour, and aesthetic reflect the dominant culture at the university; there is a sense of 'ease' and 'acceptance'. But the moment I present a persona, that is 'pro-black', 'urban', and 'intelligent', words like 'radical' and 'militant' cascade out of others' mouths, like a gushing waterfall in the Scottish Highlands.

JOSEPH: You don't think there's any truth in those labels?

TYRONE: According to whose definition?

JOSEPH: But Dr Valentine *you do* come across as quite aggressive?

TYRONE: *(Rising anger)* I'm not aggressive. I'm passionate about what I believe, and I express it that way. I'm just not prepared to accept crap, that's all.

JOSEPH: But there's ways to put yourself across.

TYRONE: That's rubbish and you know that, you come from a privileged background. You don't have to worry about your identity as it's all around us.

JOSEPH: But you're middle class too. You're not the same as the working-class students, black or white that come to this university. What's the difference between me and you?

TYRONE: *(Stern)* My identity is bound up with notions of my race and my class, shaped by a history of oppression, bias, and distortion. Therefore, my identity as a black man lingers in the shadows of the white people in this university.

JOSEPH: But you still have middle class aspirations and tendencies. You're playing semantics now Tyrone. Are you seriously expecting me to believe that you are as oppressed as your students?

TYRONE: Yes, I am. This university gives voice and influence to white people and their whiteness. My heritage is still rendered invisible on many levels. Staff, library resources, theories ...

JOSEPH: *(Interrupts)* ... but you're not part of your community either. You left that behind when you joined academia.

TYRONE: Did you leave *your* community behind?

JOSEPH: I was born middle class and white. That's a fact. I don't hide it. Whereas, you seem to deny that you're a black and middle class.

TYRONE: I'm not middle class.

JOSEPH: Who are you fooling? You might come across as radical to some of your students, but the fact is, you have a good salary, a good standard of living. You're not living your typical inner-city life. That in my opinion constitutes being middle class.

(*Tyrone goes quiet*)

(*Forceful*) This is a university. Students come here to get a degree, a job, have children, and hopefully move on to a decent life. That's all there is to it.

TYRONE: That may be the case for some students, but university is also about change and acquiring the appropriate tools to do so.

JOSEPH: But we're not talking about students. We were talking about you. You wanted me to be honest and I have been. There's nothing wrong in being middle class.

(*Tyrone's body language becomes awkward.*)

TYRONE: (*Pensive*) I was the first one in my family to get a degree, masters, and finally a doctorate. I thought it would be the ticket out of the ghetto of racist beliefs. I honestly believed it would be the key to a better life. I was wrong. That community that you mentioned, rejects me on account of being seen as middle class. The reason being is the middle classes have destroyed the community I came from. That was my motivation for coming here, to make a difference. 10 years later I'm called militant by the university and middle class by the community. It's a joke.

JOSEPH: It seems to me that you're not happy within yourself.

(*Tyrone lets out a loud sigh and paces in an agitated manner.*)

JOSEPH: (Cont'd) What does it matter who created what theories? The challenge is for students to learn how to write an essay, do a dissertation, and leave here wiser than when they came in.

TYRONE: How can our students become critical thinkers if their ideas and ways of seeing those ideas are fed to them by those who have historically and politically oppressed them?

JOSEPH: Now you're sounding radical. Why can't you accept the way things are? They're not going to change. I thought you of all people would have known that. Maybe it's time to let go of the past and just get on with it.

TYRONE: (*Rising anger*) There are so many times when I feel angry at the way the black contribution to intellectual ideas has been airbrushed out of this universities canvas, painting a picture that is almost wholly white with a few black dots dotted around the edges of the frame.

JOSEPH: There's a diverse range of people from all backgrounds here.

TYRONE: There is of course an abundance of black students, a significant amount of black technicians, catering staff, and cleaners. However, the management, lecturers, syllabi, library resources, and curriculum content remind me yet again, that diverse contributions to knowledge not only are invisible but reinforce notions of 'white privilege'.

JOSEPH: Why do you keep saying white privilege. It's not an us and them culture. You're the one citing these divisions.

TYRONE: *(Slow handclaps)* And still the power structure does not hear the call for change in academia; no-one sees the private grief of despair and no-one considers what it must feel like to still be languishing on this 'modern plantation', comprised of masters, overseers, and slaves.

JOSEPH: Modern plantation, references to slavery. What you're saying is ridiculous?

TYRONE: Being at this university tests me on every level. Most of all this university has made me question myself.

JOSEPH: Why don't you enjoy the benefits and stop taking the whole thing too seriously.

TYRONE: Why should I? Why should I struggle to gain acceptance from middle class white people like you?

JOSEPH: Now hold on a minute. It's not middle class white people who are to blame for the problems in your community.

TYRONE: It's my community now is it?

JOSEPH: *(Angry)* What about your community leaders? Where do they fit into this equation? These are individuals who on the one hand talk about self-determination, but on the other hand welcome Government handouts when they are strapped for cash. The outcome is organised chaos, personality driven community agenda's, a wilting infrastructure that seldom re-educates itself, and has little in the way of building a strong economic base. No wonder it struggles to find space to reposition itself for the greater good. But that's not this universities fault.

TYRONE: Spare me your daily mail speech. You don't represent diversity. Imagine being a senior lecturer, and still occupying a lift with a group of white men and women, where voices lower, body languages become shiftless, whilst others shuffle to one side, as if I have some kind of disease. This liberal 'colour blind' rhetoric you trundle out tries to remind me that it's all in my imagination.

JOSEPH: I'm sorry you feel like that, but taking a more radical approach won't change anything.

TYRONE: *(Upset)* Will you stop referring to me as radical?

JOSEPH: In my opinion it feels like you who's making a problem where there doesn't have to be one.

TYRONE: That's crap and you know it. Why do you have to keep hiding behind your privileged position. Why don't you express your own views? Or are you scared you might agree with me. I feel it's you who has the problem with black assertion. You need to own that.

JOSEPH: No, I don't. I don't fear black assertion. I fear that if we're not careful, this university will suffer because a few students couldn't agree over the wanton criminality of the riots.

TYRONE: Now whose being subjective.

JOSEPH: But I'm not expressing it in front of students.

TYRONE: Maybe if you did, then the students may feel that they have support from the top.

(*Professor Dawkins looks away and takes a sharp intake of breath.*)

Professor Dawkins, this caged bird (*points to himself*) at times does not sing, more of a lament or a Mississippi delta blues, about an identity that has gone and left me.

I am authentic, bright, gifted, and talented, but managing the constant loneliness and isolation, pushes fuels my sense of self-doubt.

JOSEPH: You keep talking about how things affect you here, but I don't hear you citing any examples.

TYRONE: My recent public commentary on the English Riots in Augusts is an example. I was encouraged to speak out, placed on a pedestal, only to be knocked down, by the same people who put me there.

JOSEPH: Who knocked you down?

TYRONE: I'd prefer not to say.

JOSEPH: But you're making allegations, that I feel should be substantiated.

TYRONE: All I will say is that when I did express a view that deviated from the status quo here, certain members of staff acted badly towards me.

JOSEPH: How did you know this?

TYRONE: Do you read Twitter and Facebook?

JOSEPH: No!

TYRONE: If you did, you'd know what I'm talking about?

JOSEPH: Why didn't you come and see me?

TYRONE: At this moment in time when something internally doesn't sit comfortably within my psyche and spirit I keep it to myself. Truth is, this 'inbetweenness' lingers like a bad smell. I'm sick of how this university actively uses 'colour blindness' to ensure that any expression of my own sense of blackness is locked in a darkened room, like a prisoner with a life sentence without parole.

JOSEPH: I refute what you're saying about this university. We have an excellent track record.

TYRONE: On what?

JOSEPH: We have won numerous awards and have a very successful academic track record. Plus, we attract a lot of funding to undertake ground-breaking research.

TYRONE: What about a commitment to the students who share a different worldview, need something more than being told that white people created everything.

JOSEPH: Let's not go back to this again

TYRONE: As Franz Fanon says when white people retreat into their 'whiteness', black people retreat into their 'blackness', and never the twain shall meet.

JOSEPH: Exactly. That's why we need to get beyond this black and white divide.

TYRONE: According to whose definition? You're just like the rest of your colleagues, when stuff like this happens you retreat to 'freemasonry of your race'.

JOSEPH: *(Accusatory Tone)* Don't lecture me. This university is multi-cultural. I pride myself on that position.

TYRONE: *(Sarcastic)* And still the liberal outcry masquerades as 'pseudo diversity', and then orders me to be quiet or face serious consequences. I do not want to keep defending my identity as a black man.

JOSEPH: You sound like you've got a chip on your shoulder.

TYRONE: I knew that would come up somewhere in the conversation.

JOSEPH: It's evident to me that this situation in the press could have been avoided if you'd have handled things better. What I hear is a bitter colleague who is using this situation for his own devices. Maybe you should consider your position here.

Tyrone brings out a secretly authored report and throws it across the desk. Craig has a quick scan and places it back on the desk hurriedly.

JOSEPH: What do you want me to say?

TYRONE: Explain why that report shows the attainment gap for black students in this university is 50% of that of their white counterparts?

JOSEPH: Where did you get this?

TYRONE: You don't need to know. I'd like you to explain it.

JOSEPH: I don't have to explain anything.

TYRONE: As I thought. You wanted to push the universities so called excellent track record in my face and when I show you some evidence to support my argument, you want to push it to one side.

JOSEPH: This report has nothing to do with the allegations.

TYRONE: It has everything to do with the allegations. The evidence in this report demonstrates categorically that this university has been failing black students over a period of time and now you want to blame the students. To me, you're a hypocrite, with no backbone. You stated very clearly in the beginning of this conversation that you had an obligation to your students. Where is it now then, tell me?

JOSEPH: I don't have to sit here and take this.

TYRONE: Why not, you've been ramming it down my throat since I came in. Admit it, you're a tired old white man, that can't see that we're living in a new time. You need to smell the coffee and see what's in front of your face.

JOSEPH: *(Explodes)* Okay I do feel a threat from the way things are now. I've never been a supporter of multi-culturalism, anti-racism, or equal opportunities. I fear many of us are losing their place in the world. And I fear that people like yourself are going to make things worse. Unlike you, I've tried to champion my causes quietly

Leaving some of my own subjectivity behind for the sake of this university and contrary to popular belief, the students. What I find distasteful is when the inmate start running the asylum. *(Composes himself and calms down.)*

(There is an uncomfortable silence.)

Because of this scandal I may be forced to resign.

(*Lengthy silence punctuated by Professor Dawkins struggling with keeping his emotions in. He lets out a deep sigh and turns his head away as if he's crying. He gets to his feet and paces nervously.*)

(*Angry*) I've been involved in education for almost 40 years. I've taught at all levels, degree, masters, supervised PhD's, and ended up running several departments. I've always tried my best to get on with everyone. And somehow looking at this situation I'm reminded how things have changed. In my day students had respect for each other, didn't fight, and channelled their energies into getting a decent job and contributing to society.

(*Lengthy silence.*)

TYRONE: You and I both know you can't stand in the way of progress. I'm sure one day both of our ideas will be confined to history. I take no great pleasure in what's happening. But this issue is bigger than the both of us. You know that.

JOSEPH: But what happened to the days when education meant something. I mean, this generation is too caught up in technology fast living. When I was young it was never like that.

TYRONE: So, there were no rebels or those who questioned when you were at university?

JOSEPH: (*Sighs*) Who am I trying to kid? We were rebellious, in our own way. I suppose deep down I could do without this type of situation. I'm close to retirement. I don't need the stress.

TYRONE: Who does?

JOSEPH: Maybe you're right. Maybe I should bow out gracefully. (*To himself.*) What's gone wrong? So, where does this leave us?

(*Tyrone pulls an envelope from his bag and hands it to Professor Dawkins, who opens it and scans it quickly.*)

JOSEPH: Where will you go?

TYRONE: Years ago a friend of mine said if you're going to struggle, struggle in the sun. I've just resigned from my post and am going to take up a new position at the University of the West Indies in the next semester.

JOSEPH: I'm really sorry to hear about that. I hope it's not this situation that's made you want to leave.

TYRONE: Any good performer knows when to get off stage. I'm not prepared to go through what my father went through and feel like a salmon swimming up stream.

JOSEPH: But what about the students, your community, and more importantly this university.

TYRONE: Let's be honest Professor Dawkins, you and I both know that this university is stuck. I don't want to continue to fight all the time. I'm tired of the label radical and militant. I want to be somewhere, where people look like me and I don't have to explain or justify myself. It's that simple.

JOSEPH: But it sounds like you're giving in.

TYRONE: No, I'm not. I'm just choosing to fight a different battle, that's all. *(Looks at his watch.)* Look I've got to go.

JOSEPH: Look, I know this conversation didn't got off to a good start, but I do want to thank you for opening my eyes. I don't know if I will be able to do anything substantial, but I'm grateful for the time we've spent. I know you must feel that I'm old fashioned, which I'm sure is disappointing to you. If I'm being honest, I know I'm a man of my time and a lot of what I believe is not relevant anymore. I just have a hard time accepting it. It's not a justification, merely an explanation. If I had the courage like you, maybe I would leave too. I fear I'm too old for that now.

TYRONE: You're never too old. Listen, you take care.

(Professor Dawkins takes a long hard look at Tyrone, as he exits quietly. Professor Dawkins gets to his feet and stares out the window. A call comes through.)

(To the audience) An interesting conversation with someone from Zimbabwe recently was a real blessing, when helping understand where I'm now at. He said that it is better to be someone who prefers to light a candle in a darkened room, rather than shout at the same darkened room for not being dark enough. What do you think? *(Exits.)*

THE END

On watching this theatrical rendition of my reflexive journey, I was in a position to stand back from my subjective feelings, and begin to reassess some of own thoughts about my journey. Not only did I feel validated but some much-needed healing also took place. On talking to the audience during a lively question and answer session I was in a position to draw on their perceptions of my journey that also facilitated some of reflexivity, similar to having a supervisory session with colleagues. I am very aware that not every researcher is confident to present their story in this way. Therefore, for those researchers who are keen to explore their own selves in this way this next section will hopefully provide some steer when looking at some of the key considerations when **performing auto–ethnographically**.

Performing auto-ethnographically

Denzin (2018) argues that performing auto-ethnographically must be taken seriously. To do so the researcher must embrace and immerse themselves fully in the world of their research, combined with finding the vernacular that is befitting to the work itself. In essence each research needs to find their 'auto-ethnographic' voice. Much the same as the TEDx format that requires many performative elements that each speaker must grapple with, so must presenting the researchers own narrative experiences.

- **Know your story:** Knowing your story is not just about memorizing the content. It is about understanding the world of story, its characters, the hidden meanings, and more importantly the key themes and messages contained within the story as a whole. Failure to do will result in an audience either not getting the message or losing interest if the story meanders and goes off track.

- **What is the mood of the story:** As the storyteller your responsibility is to make your story fresh, interesting, vibrant, and certainly not predictable. If you have studied your story well you will be able to create the mood much the same as an orchestra does with music. Remember you are in charge of shaping the overall direction of your personal narrative.
- **Act naturally:** Gestures add interest and emphasis to your story. If you're nervous, feel awkward or stilted; start slowly and add movements or gestures as you begin to relax. Practice gestures as part of your story preparation and they'll come easier when you present.
- **Make eye contact:** A great way to help calm your nerves is to make eye contact with one person in the audience. Speak only to them. When you've looked at them long enough to feel you've made a connection, move on to another person, and then another. One of the best ways to keep your audience engaged in your story is to maintain good eye contact.
- **Show your feelings:** You may normally be reserved, but for your story, open with a smile. Show your audience you're happy to share your information with them. Facial expressions add power to your words. Just be sure your expressions are appropriate to your subject matter.
- **Make yourself heard:** There are several aspects of verbal delivery to consider. Volume is probably the most important. Make sure you speak loudly enough so that everyone can hear you. If you're not sure, ask. Also, consider your rate of delivery. When presenters are nervous they often speak faster. Try to speak slowly and clearly, so your audience can understand every word. Finally, consider the pitch of your voice. Too much variation is distracting. Too little is monotonous. Aim for consistency with some variation when it's appropriate to the content.
- **Be energetic:** One thing I have learned is an enthusiastic storyteller will get a standing ovation, applause, and appreciation. An audience wants to get excited, enthused, challenged, and entertained all at the same time. If you understand the mood, temperament, and tempo of your story, you should be able to pace yourself and the energy required to have the maximum impact on your audience.
- **Become the characters:** If your story contains numerous characters it is critical for you to present their traits, mannerisms, gestures, and differences, as a way of enabling the audience to know who's who in the story. Failure to do so will lose the audience. So being clear in your presentation will greatly add to the experience of the audience, as well as ensuring you get your message across.
- **Make it interesting:** Simple as this sounds making a story interesting requires great skill. It requires you the storyteller to gauge the mood of the audience and to match the delivery to ensure there is a satisfactory outcome. To ensure you make the story interesting, you must lose yourself in the world of the

story. If you are nervous or too self-conscious you can inhibit the overall tone of the story which may come across as boring or uninteresting.

Important here is to develop strong '**presentation literacy**'. What makes good 'presentation literacy?' What is it that captivates the imagination, makes us gasp in amazement, sigh with relief, cry with sadness, howl with laughter, or be totally confused by a trick ending? A strong and robust presentation can solve problems, and give insight/s into the complexities of our lives. Having undertaken a TEDx talk early in 2018, I was introduced to the idea of 'presentation literacy' as a key component of navigating the complexity of sharing our personal story. For researchers who engage fully in reflexive practice presentation literacy is not only an important consideration when sharing with audiences, but it can also generate more soft impacts with your audience. The following is merely a guide, not a definitive list of pointers that emerged from my preparation for doing my TEDx talk:

- **PRESENT with passion:** If there is no passion the audience will switch off quickly. Your job is to emotionally connect to the audience from the moment you step onto the stage. Therefore, a strong entrance is essential. Important here is maintaining and sustaining your energy, drive, and enthusiasm throughout. Emotional impact will always get the audience on your side.
- **KNOW your audience:** Knowing your audience requires you to do your background research. Failure to do so will result in reducing your overall impact, which in turn will damage your presentation. If want to excite, motivate, inspire, and transform your audience, understanding who they are, what they want, and what you want from them beforehand is a good strategy for success.
- **OPEN correctly:** One of the first rules when doing stand-up comedy or spoken word is having a 'good opening'. The opening sets the tone for the presentation and must convey exactly what you intend to do by 'appropriate signposts'. It is important that you guide the audience in ways that will enable them to be clear about your intent.
- **CONNECT with your audience:** At times the audience's attention can wander, be disengaged, or at worst disinterested. There are numerous reasons why this happens. It is important to push through the 'dead moments' and come out on top. Your job is to 'work the room' maintaining control and composure at all times.
- **RESPECT your audience:** In every presentation there are moments when things don't go well, which can be off putting and upsetting. However, at no stage should you disrespect your audience. Conflict can be handled better by learning how to improvise much the same way that stand-up comedians deal with 'hecklers'.
- **TELL a good story:** Remember you are doing a presentation, not delivering a lecture. Lectures are very formal affairs and require a delivery style where facts and other related information can be passed on. If you're wanting an audience to engage with you then tell stories that are relevant, appropriate, and engaging. Make sure they are rich with anecdotes, insights, and wisdom.

- **SHOW us something we need to know:** With the amount of information on TV, social media, and the internet many of us suffer from 'information overload'. Therefore, it is vital for you to try and find new, innovative, and creative ways to tell us things we need to know. Feed the audience's hunger for experiences that takes them to new points of understanding.
- **RISK is the art of surprise:** Nothing's worse than listening to someone who is boring, where the presentation is predictable, mundane, and dry. Magicians are always full of surprises, while a good thriller contains twists and turns. Your presentation should involve elements of surprise to take the audience off guard. To do requires you to take some risks.
- **IMPACT with a smile:** When I go to the dentist, hospital, or a funeral, I expect professionals to personable in spite of doing a difficult job. As presenters it is important to recognise that audiences are not stupid and will be able to read your emotions. If you look disinterested, they will switch off. Don't be frightened to engage your audience with humour even if you're tackling a difficult and complex subject or issue.
- **BRICOLEUR not Saboteur:** Don't be satisfied to rely purely on your voice to carry your message to the audience. We live in an age which is much more sophisticated. Audiences expect an 'experience' not just a straightforward 'presentation' consisting of one or two elements. Be multi-faceted in your approach. Make it as sensory as possible.
- **LESS is more:** Ted Talks famously gives presenters 18 minutes. I personally love the concept that emerges from the Caribbean called 'liming'. Liming basically means chilling out and relaxing, where conversations last as long as they're supposed to. An experienced presenter and storyteller gauges the audience's mood, doesn't overstay their welcome, and works towards a timely exit, which doesn't exhaust the audience.
- **WISDOM is the destination:** If you've set up your story well, delivered it with clarity, engaged your audience, maintained the energy, and concluded in a way that leaves everyone wanting more, then you have managed to stay on the right lane. If you have done that, then the wisdom has been imparted. This in turn means you would have successfully generated some kind of impact.

In 2010, I undertook a Winston Churchill International Travel Fellowship where the aim was to look at models of good practice where addressing fatherlessness, father hunger, and father deficit among young men has created stronger communities. One encounter I had with a gang member taught me a painful but valuable lesson, when for the first time, I 'went native'. In participant observation research, **going native** means becoming so involved with and sympathetic to the group, the researcher loses objectivity. The following reflection on the encounter highlights the problems I faced, and how performance aided me in making sense of what I'd done that nearly jeopardised my research overall.

Going native, spontaneous poetics, and Bu

Night has descended; 'T' and I are in a car park, face-to-face with a man sporting a red bandana. My first encounter with a member of the 'Bloods' gang is surreal, challenging, and insightful. Being granted an audience with him, followed by a meeting I will never forget was one of the most powerful experiences of my life. He was charismatic, intelligent, and truly a leader. The conversation did not focus on gangs, but more on fatherhood and society in general. The mixture of fear and exhilaration ran through my veins. All the way through the conversation I wondered about his childhood, dreams, aspirations, and what led him into such a lifestyle. Bu felt less of an avenging angel and more as someone who decided that a history of oppression and limited life chance for a suffering community gave him a mandate to operate in opposition to the forces of law and order. In some respect it felt like an act of defiance with menace and consequences. Eventually, I plucked up the courage to ask him how I could prevent my own son from joining a gang. He quickly told me that if I stayed at home with him, ensured he was loved, combined with supporting his education, he would escape the lure of gang life. I concluded by asking Bu if it was all worth it. To my shock, he lifted up his shirt, to reveal a mass of bullet holes, and then calmly said, 'What do you think?' The meeting ended, Bu went on his way, and I was back sitting next to 'T', where we began to debrief. I was truly impressed not only by 'T's unswerving commitment to trying to make Baltimore a better place, but the gang member's openness to reasoning and dialogue. Be under no illusion, any male US gang member is no saint. However, they are men and fathers, who have made a choice that many find offensive, scary, and wrong. Be that as it may, they exist alongside us, occupying the same space, going to the same shops, taking their kids to school, and trying to survive in their own way. We can all have an opinion, view or judgement as to what is right and wrong. What I would say is, until you have stood face to face with someone like the guy I have just met, we will continue to believe the hype and moral panic that surrounds gang culture. Yes, they are menacing individuals who have done all sorts of stuff. The truth is that the solution for changing them will not be found in more incarceration, biased media coverage, or ignoring their existence. Gangs are a complex social phenomenon that requires more than just rhetorical posturing to sort it out. I don't have the solution, but what I did learn today, is that it starts with dialogue. But first you have to gain access. That access was created by 'T'. The sad fact remains there are many guys like 'T', who don't get paid, supported, and validated for what they do. Yet he saves as many lives as any paramedic or surgeon. After 12 hours on the road 'T' says he will drop me home. Suddenly an incident involving five white police officers arresting a young black woman forces 'T' to stop, pull over, take out a video camera and record what they're doing. 'T' archives stuff that happens on the streets as he wants to make a documentary on the abuses that take place on a regular basis. Lo and behold, it is taking place opposite Little Melvin's shop front. We stop off and talk with Little Melvin for about an hour before making our way home. I am thoroughly exhausted and take several hours to decompress reground myself. Angry at myself for letting myself get too close to the issue I had a massive headache and was very restless. However, I remember reading the works of beat poet Jack Kerouac who developed 'spontaneous prose' which is a lay person's term for writing a stream of consciousness. Similarly, I underwent a similar exercise using (spontaneous) data verbalization, which I titled **achin'**. Achin' symbolizes the feelings I had knowing I had 'gone native'.

Achin'

Frustrated ... berated ... I stated ... clearly
The terms ... like worms ... things turn
Then burn ... with scorn ... ain't born ... with a spoon
In my mouth ... it happens like lightnin' ...
It's frightenin' ... how it comes
'N' goes ... then flows ... then shows ... itself
Like a demon ... rips yer heart out ... shout
Stout ... like wood ... no I'm not ... hit the spot ... where ... care ...
Fear ... got nuff ... what stuff ... ain't a bluff
Too ruff ... on the cusp ... or verge ... of a breakdown
Taken down ... that's me ... do you see ... me ... no you don't
I'm here ... then there ... I'm here ... not there
Where do you want ...
Want who ... me ... don't you see
Or believe ... that stream ... or dream
Consciousness ... need to redress ... the ache ...
As it takes ... my soul ... placed in the hole
On the roll ... er coaster ... flyin'
Back 'n' forth ... forth 'n' back ...
Crack ... slap ... clap ... rise ... fall ...
Bawl ... like a child ... mild like soap
In yer eyes ... always tries to please ... the disease
Infects ... connects ... rejects my soul's need ...
Can't feed ... my spirit ... kill it ... fill it
Trippin' 'n' fallin' 'n' rantin' 'n' stallin'
What the ... what the ... what the ...
Confusion. .. infusion of ideas ... with the
Fears I wrestle ... with self ... poor health
Head pounds ... dead sounds ... rebounds
Become a clown ... feelin' down ... can't raise

Dark blue haze ... crazed ... laughter inside ...
tried ... nearly died ... slip 'n' slide
What the ... what the ... what the ...
K ... k ... k ... white knights in flight ...
The plight of the Black man is
Nothing other than himself ... face it ... place it ...
Re-frame ... re-name ... re-claim
All that is yours ... the choice ... your voice ...
Is silent ... violent ... no mild ... like a child ... you're mashed
You've crashed ... flashed
Pain in the face of
Love ... like a glove ... it don't fit right ... hold it tight.
Blind no sight ... taken flight ... refuge ... refuse
Diffuse ... accuse ... who me ...
What the ... what the ... what the ...
Is going on INSIDE MY HEAD

On first reflection what I had written didn't make sense. However, the importance of using spontaneous reflexivity like this was to try and reduce the level of control over how I was feeling. The resulting outcome captured an instant response to my self-reflection. Mills (1959) feels that whatever methodology is used, the researcher should be a good craftsperson. In doing so, Mills argues that researchers should avoid any rigid set of procedures and seek to develop and to use the sociological imagination. Mills feels that the conventions of research methods can limit envisioning ways of knowing and seeing that will contest conventional wisdom. In this case I used the experience of going native to use performance as a way of 'taking to myself' making myself accountable for the mistake I made. In performing and hearing my testimony I was reminded how emotionally impacting the whole experience was.

Struggling with Mikey

In another case, I undertook some case study research with a young man at risk. Aware that I was ethically bound not to divulge to the subject of the case study the results of my observations, I felt awkward and uncomfortable by what I felt was quite deceitful. After all I was writing about someone's life. The resulting outcome was to produce an auto-ethnographic poem that emerged from the following case study 'Mikey':

Case study (extract)

I sit waiting in a small living room located in a children's home anticipating the arrival of Mikey, a young man in the care of the Nottingham Youth Offending team. I learn that Mikey is on the cusp of serious offending. After a short wait Mikey surfaces wearing pyjama bottoms, sporting a bare chest, with large head of hair on show. Mikey reveals he is 15 years of age and of mixed parentage. Mikey is slim and has no battle scars over his body. Mikey further reveals he has grown up with his grandmother, didn't finish school, has spent time growing up in care, and acknowledges that his offending is becoming problematic. My first impressions of Mikey is that of an insular, angry, and potentially volatile young man who is crying out for support, but emotionally struggling to ask for it. Mikey's body language, tone of voice, and general demeanour suggests that he is weary of meeting yet another 'professional stranger' where his first line of attack/defence is to suss me out. I know if I am to get through to him I will need to tread lightly, listen intently, and be measured in my approach, in a calm and relaxed way. Rolling with the punches is all part of the initial 'getting to know you' phase of a young man like Mikey.

Ice breaker

Mikey and I swap stories that breaks the ice which then creates a tipping point for a connection where the wisdom says just 'keep it real'. Initially Mikey tells me I am just another vested interest wanting to pick his brain and make some bogus recommendations in a report that no one is going to read or act on. After a grilling about my motivation the conversation settles down where I continue to press Mikey about his health and well-being, which he acknowledges with the occasional fiery and intense answer. I become very aware of the difficulty Mikey finds in talking openly based on his lack of trust of anyone or anything in authority. It is at that point I decide to pull back and give Mikey the space to engage with me on his own terms as pushing Mikey into a corner may result in conflict that I wanted to avoid. A few minutes pass and Mikey sits in silence as he is still fearful of opening himself up to me. Then out of nowhere Mikey begins to open up. For over an hour we engaged in deep discussion about the things that were troubling him. Mikey reveals many things about his distress, the strained relationship with his parents; the pain of not experiencing love in his life; his sister's incarceration; the relationship with his grandmother; all underpinned by a deep sense of loss and despair in relation to his life in general.

Code of the streets

Mikey's tough exterior drops off him like snow on a melting glacier. I was now talking to someone who was less of a 'bad boy' or 'young offender', but a young man in need of understanding and love. My mission was to map the journey travelled by Mikey to assess the impact of his behaviour on his aspirations and life in general. First observations would suggest he is flourishing, confident, and in control of his life. Probing deeper it's clear that Mikey is merely coping, managing, and surviving. Mikey possesses a strong awareness of his situation and locates his lived reality; fear of intimacy, lack of trust, experiences of poverty, engagement with violence, the battle with his on-going, continuous pain, struggling with his losses, and so on. However, he does have aspirations; wants a chance, and a strong desire to do well. Listening to Mikey it's easy to forget that he lives in a restricted environment, faces oppressive forces such as street violence, and is constantly exposed to a crumbling inner-city infrastructure. It is clear that Mikey has been involved in anti-social behaviour and crime.

Poor socialization

In the initial assessment process, it is evident that how he sees themselves and has been shaped by a history of poor socialization and blocked opportunities. The cumulative impact of those experiences has resulted in a distorted and confused sense of personal identity. Mikey displays a range of personal attitudes and perspectives that would suggest he has been impacted by a significant amount of personal and social neglect that has manifested in him projecting a negative self-concept. The absence of strong social bonds, poor parenting, systemic neglect, an inability to find inner peace, combined with many fractured relationships has led Mikey to develop a nihilistic mind set. The net result of the above list is a further display and projection of a range of behaviours that fuels other negative personal traits he has cultivated.

Community disconnect

Mikey talks openly about being disconnected from his family, the wider community, and society at large, where the 'streets' has now become the escape from which he finds solace and a space to operate in 'stealth. Unable to form strong and safe social bonds, Mikey forms alliances with others involved in anti-social behaviour and criminal activity, referred to as 'differential association'. Essentially, some of Mikey's behaviour is learned from his 'association/s' with other criminals. As the pressure to forge alliances creates more internal conflicts, Mikey goes through moments of 'confusion' based on having split loyalties. Important here is in the recognition that in spite of what Mikey portrays he is both vulnerable and susceptible to the influence of others, and will be tempted to 'follow the crowd' as a way of seeking approval and fitting in. Failure to intervene at the point when Mikey enters into the 'confused stage' of his 'life course' will create more stress and inner turmoil.

Pressure

The pressure coming from family, peers, the streets, and society at large, will also push him in many directions. If the alternatives to stay on the right path are not accessible or are blocked, then Mikey will continue to engage with anti-social and criminal options available to him. Mikey's negative side is contrasted with a significant amount of confidence and sensitivity in the way he articulates his story. This side of his character clearly demonstrates Mikey's potential to transcend his current status as an offender. This in my view reveals some positive traits that needs to be acknowledged. At this stage it is important to work with Mikey supporting him to explore all options available to him. Supporting Mikey's potential, dreams, and aspirations, alongside building his confidence and self-esteem are critical factors in enabling him to engage fully in those things required for both personal change and developing a more pro-social identity. It is my view that once Mikey begins to experience the positive benefits of a new-found sense of identity, he may begin to develop the tools to make different and more informed choices that are tied to who, not what, he is as a young man.

Acceptance

Self-acceptance for Mikey is less about professionals such as myself forcing him to be complaint, but more of empowering him to become the 'author of his own life' and to steer his own ship. Important here is to look at Mikey and his relationship to criminality. The following is a list of some of my observations emerging from our discussions. It is important to state from the outset that the following list of observations are not proven but reflective of the subject of the conversations we were having. It is clearly evident that 'Mikey's age and his growing engagement with, connection to, the streets, criminal activity, and anti-social behaviour may at some stage disable his ability to stay 'crime free'. A prevalent feature of many young people is in the way in which the 'code of the streets' creates a 'survival of the fittest' mentality. This 'code of the streets' tends to revolve around the ability to navigate the perils of violence, gang culture, drugs, and extreme social deprivation. Individuals who understood and could manage the 'code of the street', would use extreme menace and intimidation to control who could access to the code. As those interviewed highlighted the there are no hard and fast rules about survival on the streets, other than you have to survive at all costs.

The future

Not thinking about the future, would suggest that the 'code of the streets' is less about planning a future, or looking back, but more of living in the moment, as you never know what is around the corner. Mikey saw the streets as a place to have some control over his life and in spite of being a dangerous space to occupy, gave him some purpose. Mikey talked openly about the desire to get off the streets but as occupation of that space demands loyalty there are very few exist strategies. By and large he sees himself as soldier, defending his territory. By equating his role as soldiers, it could be argued that Mikey internalizes and expresses a performance as an alternative police force, designed to keep order in their communities, with a strong sense of duty and loyalty. Death seemed to be casually accepted norm which revealed a darker truth, 'kill or be killed'.

Desistance

Achieving desistance is often very difficult and requires the building of both human and social capital. This would suggest that this type of intervention required for young offenders needs to promote his individual's goods as well as managing and reducing any risks posed. A major aim of rehabilitative work is to enable individuals like Mikey to develop a life plan that involves ways of effectively securing primary human goods without harming others. However, this is not just about tackling risk factors; it is about the holistic reconstruction of the self that requires practitioners to consider and address individual, relational and contextual factors; attending to both personal characteristics and social environments. The structural context of most young offenders lived reality and the level of social disorganisation within the community is at the core of the problems faced by them relation to his desistance trajectory. Many of them could benefit from a process referred to as 'knifing off'.

Knifing off

'Knifing off' is about the means by which individuals like Mikey are thought to change their lives by severing themselves from detrimental environments. It is also important to consider the influence of local cultures and how membership of powerful street cultures fractures the possibility of desistance in inner city communities. Before young men are willing to give up their working identity as a lawbreaker, they must begin to perceive this identity as unsatisfying, thus weakening his commitment to it. Unless the participants are embedded into new social networks that not only supports a new identity and tastes but can also isolate him from those who would oppose them quitting crime or induce him to continue in his criminal ways, then desistance is highly unlikely. These aspirations are built on two premises: firstly, all the young men have skills, abilities and talents that can and should be used for the benefit of the community; and secondly, that rather than seeing them as 'community liabilities', the communities needs to view, enlist and deploy them, as 'community assets'.

Assets or liability?

Enabling and supporting young men like Mikey to desist is about providing them with what has been missing from their lives. To promote a successful, positive change the community must target their negative value system in ways that will increase their appreciation for the challenges facing the communities they have affected, connected to real and meaningful opportunities. However, the increasingly rising 'hyper-masculine' stance suggests that at this moment in time they are unwilling to consider a shift in his personal identity for fear of losing control of aspects of their lives which they don't trust. Many of the participants require a 'safe space' to work out their anxieties, frustrations, and difficulties if they are to successfully reintegrate back into the community. They need encouragement, opportunities and structures through which he can function as full and bona fide member of the community and make a positive contribution to community life. Understanding their health and well-being issues/concerns should involve listening and hearing their 'stories'. If these young people cannot fulfil their potential based on the erosion of his self-concept it is questionable whether they can maintain a focus that will enable them to desist from crime. The inability of young men like Mikey to experience; friendship, community, happiness, agency and inner peace means he will continue to operate in a high state of hyper vigilance that will make necessary interventions more problematic.

Discussions

Much of today's discussions around young offenders are cast in terms of public safety, recidivism and law enforcement. However, future dialogue around the understandings of his desistance must locate its vision around investigating how rehabilitative processes can create greater opportunities for him to reduce the possibility of re-offending. There needs to be a shifting emphasis of service delivery for young offenders, away from diagnosis and prescriptions, to screening, accurate assessment and identification of immediate needs. A service or practitioners that do not see, acknowledge, or understand the impact of fractured social bonds and poor socialisation on young men will only serve to perpetuate the difficulties that he experiences. The result was 'beyond the wall'. After I had submitted the case study to the youth offending service I reconnected with the young man who was the subject of my research. As it wasn't appropriate to share my findings with him, I instead shared a 'data verbalization' story with him that emerged from deconstructing the case study, extracting the key themes, and constructing the piece around those themes. In sharing it with him I made my reflexive account available to him. The result was to strengthen our connection.

Beyond the wall

> Precious moments like this
> Are all we have to bind us
> To each other
> Empty memories are filled with new thoughts
> As we smile together
> For the first time
> Like innocent children
> Learnin' a new game
> Fragments of a broken past
> Pieced together
> To heal our pain
> Which we reveal thru'
> Glazed eyes 'n' silent tears

We become men
Brothaz on the same journey
Who have trod the different paths
But today
We see the same things
Dream the same dreams
'N' escape into a secret world of
Laughter 'n' celebration
Thru' the darkness comes light
Thru' the light we step together
Holdin' on to the time we have left
Then the flow is broken
We embrace … you leave
'N' I shed a tear
As the remnants of those moments
Evaporate like steam
I stand outside the prison walls
'N' look back
I say, "Look beyond the wall brotha …
Look beyond the wall

Speaking your truth

Qualitative interviewing involves a continuous process of reflection on the research. 'Reflexivity' is the process of examining both oneself as researcher, and the research relationship. As stated previously reflexivity involves examining one's 'conceptual baggage' 'assumptions' and 'preconceptions' and how these affect research decisions. Doing this enables personal thoughts, feelings, stories, and observations to give a greater understanding of the social context which is being studied. Auto ethnography as Denzin (2018) argues must always be interventionist, seeking to give notice to those who may not be allowed to tell their story or who are denied a voice to speak. Autoethnographers must therefore reveal their total interaction within the research setting by exposing their subjective experiences, both the personal and the political. Using this approach therefore is a 'critical response' to the awkwardness of the researcher's experiences generated by research practices that do not validate the 'subjective experiences' of the researcher. Important here is how performing auto-ethnography can give participants of the research inquiry a deeper insight into the researcher's experiences, processes, and methods, as a way of increasing the participatory nature of the research itself. In doing so, the researcher demonstrates their own positioning in an open and transparent manner. In order to assess the overall impact of myself as researcher on the subjects of the inquiry, alongside their impact on the researcher, the use of reflexivity is important always. One of the biggest conflicts in relation to 'on road' research is that of 'reliability' and 'validity'. Reliability is the consistency of a result over time (Babbie, 2002).

Results over time

The use of a quantitative method is more likely to generate results that are consistent over time, as a result of the controlled environment and the standardization that may arise from standardization in testing. Chilisa (2012) on the other hand argues that all research methodologies should centre on the concerns and worldviews of the research subjects so that they understand themselves through their own assumptions and perspectives. Mills (1959) so too sees that whatever methodology is used the researcher should be a good craftsman: In doing so, Mills argues that researchers should avoid any rigid set of procedures and seek to develop and to use the sociological imagination. Mills feels that the conventions of research methods can limit envisioning ways of knowing and seeing that will contest conventional wisdom. Likewise, Goffman (1959) argues during the period in which the individual is in the immediate presence of the others, few events may occur which directly provide the others with the conclusive information they will need if they are to direct wisely their own activity. Denzin (2010) also argues that mixed methods are important inasmuch as they assist the researcher to confront and work through the epistemological, methodological and ethical stance toward critical inquiry each generation must offer its responses to current and past criticisms. Important as all of the previous views are, a key question is missed out. Namely, for whose benefit is the research? Understandably, research emerges out a need to create meaning through investigation of social phenomena. The responsibility is mainly entrusted to the academy that is supposed to operate with objectivity, fairness, and have the necessary medicine to remedy the illnesses before them. However, sometimes communities under pressure need those of us who are on the spot to give them feedback in ways that will solve a problem that happened 'on the spot', as well as making some sense out of what has just happened. Creating a 'performative safe space' to share my auto-ethnographic experiences is designed to make the research process open and transparent. Spence (2010) sees this safe space as serving an important function where the researcher does not have to defend their existence or humanity (Spence, 2010: 68). Many black men I encounter express reservations not only about working with 'insensitive researchers' based on previous experiences of being 'researched on' and criticise those methods that are exclusive not inclusive. They also frequently express the importance of having a researcher who comes from a similar background to their own. Overall, my participants express appreciation with the approach I take. It is also very evident that many black men who have been to prison and have re-entered the community need a similar safe space to voice and share their experiences, free from the judgement and suspicion. The term used by both community participants and the prisoners to describe this type of interaction is 'keepin' it real'. Not only does 'keepin' it real' create and build trust, but also it validates their sense of worth and boosts their self-esteem. The occupation of space free from racialized judgements is an important consideration for all of those who take part in research that involves auto-ethnographic reflections.

Guiding assumptions

The lack of culturally competent approaches when researching with black men in research has implications for research as a whole (Brookes, Glynn, & Wilson, 2012). Mertens (2007) so too argues all researchers should be cognizant of the philosophical and political assumptions that guide their work. For many black men in research, negative experiences they encounter from researchers has also damaged the confidence they had in a world where their views have been distorted in the name of criminal justice research. Creating an environment that is safe and relaxing is a crucial part of the dialogue with black men. A recurring question: why should researcher's working outside the box accept notions of subordination just because they are using innovative and creative research methods, theories, and analysis? Furthermore, why does this type of oppression seemingly pass off without question or challenge? A history of racial subordination clearly makes me as a non-white researcher more vigilant and defiant in the face of continuing and sustainable pressure coming from forces designed to keep me down. One explanation could be that as black researchers, qualified as we are, we are also rendered powerless in an academic system that privileges one group over another, which does not provide us with a sense of equal justice in terms of validating both our research and the methods we employ.

Dominant narratives

How then do progressive researchers maintain the balance between challenging the status quo, whilst at the same time not being sucked in to the very machinery that grinds your energy down? The inability of criminologists who suffer racial disparities in the criminal justice research domain to successfully operate independently of street level bureaucrats, policy makers, and strategic agencies is also problematic and may require a new approach that determines its own destiny. Central to this proposition is in the way my personal narrative is produced and produces change. The dominant narrative that restricts and renders my 'counter narratives' invisible needs to cease. Regardless of the exclusion zone that surrounds the loneliness of the long-distance researcher I continue to strive and struggle for validation, not just in the eyes of those who oppress us, but from those who see the abilities of the progressive researcher as part of a remedy leading towards transformation and liberation. The future for researching communities should involve listening and hearing the researcher's counter-narrative/s that must address itself to the process of both social and political change. It may be that progressive researchers have to re-frame what is right for themselves. By the right to narrate I mean to suggest the creation of a space where progressive researchers are free to represent themselves. This is a process which involves seeing ourselves less as outsiders in academia and more of experiencing our research experience from differing perspectives, not defined according to the dictates of other privileged positions. As many researchers are situated differently in relation to the economic, political, and social worlds of academic research and funding, maybe a unification of progressive researchers is now required. This would enable independent approaches and visions to grow and become relevant to this area of the inner city where I reside. Similarly, to the view expressed by Mienczakowski (2000) I too feel it is probably now time for progressive researchers seeking wider impacts, through performance works, to adjust their outlook from construction of textual representation to the implications and power of performed representations.

Summary

This chapter focussed on some of the practical considerations regarding performing 'autoethnography' and 'reflexivity'. It was intended to give researchers an insight into my own journey in relation to presenting my subjective experiences as a researcher by using case examples of my approach using methods such as:

- Ethnodrama
- Spontaneous poetics
- Spoken word
- Data verbalization

Reflection questions

1. What role does reflexivity play in your own research practice?
2. How important is presenting reflexivity using a performative approach?

References

Alvesson, M. & Skoldberg, K. (2009) *Reflexive Methodology: New Vistas for Qualitative Research*, London: Sage.
Babbie, E. (2002) *The Basics of Social Research*, Belmont, CA: Wadsworth Publishing.
Becker, H. (1963) *Outsiders: Studies in Sociology and Deviance*, New York: Free Press.
Becker, H. (1967) 'Whose side are we on?', *Social Problems*, 14: 239–247.
Brookes, M., Glynn, M., & Wilson, D. (2012) 'Black men, therapeutic communities and HMP Grendon', *The International Journal of Therapeutic Communities*, 33(1): 16–26.
Brown, L. & Strega, S. (2005) *Research as Resistance: Critical, Indigenous, and Anti-Oppressive Approaches*, Ontario: Canadian Scholars Press/Women's Press.
Carstensen-Egwuom, I. (2013) 'Connecting intersectionality and reflexivity: Methodological approaches to social positionalities', *Erkunde*, 68(4): 265–276.
Chang, H. (2008). *Autoethnography as Method*, Walnut Creek, CA: Left Coast Press.
Chilisa, B. (2012) *Indigenous research methodologies*, London: Sage.
DeFrantz, T.F. & Gonzalez, A. (2014) *Black Performance Theory*, London: Duke University Press.
Denzin, N.K. (2010) *The Qualitative Manifesto*, Walnut Creek, CA: Left Coast Press.
Denzin, N.K. & Giardana, M. (2017) *Qualitative Inquiry in Neo Liberal Times*, New York: Routledge.
Denzin, N.K. (2018) *Performance Autoethnography: Critical Pedagogy and the politics of culture*, London: Sage.

Dunbar, P. (1892) *Lyrics of a Lowly Life*, New York: Citadel Press.

Duneier, M. (2006) 'Voices from the sidewalk: ethnography and writing race', *Ethnic and Racial Studies*, 29(3): 543–565.

Ellingsworth, L. (2017) *Embodiment in Qualitative Research*, Oxford: Routledge.

Emirbayer, M. & Desmond, M. (2012) 'Race and reflexivity', *Ethnic and Racial Studies* 35(4): 574–599.

Goffman, E. (1959) *The Presentation of Self in Everyday Life*, London: Penguin.

McAdams, D. (1988) *Power, Intimacy, and the Life Story*, London: Guilford Press.

Mauthner, N.S. & Doucet, A. (2003) 'Reflexive accounts and accounts of reflexivity in qualitative data analysis', *Sociology*, 37(3): 413–431.

Mead, H. (1932) *The Philosophy of the Present*, London: Open Court Publishing.

Mertens, D. (2007) 'Transformative paradigm: Mixed methods and social justice', *Journal of Mixed Methods Research*, 1(3): 212–225.

Mills, C.W. (1959) *The Sociological Imagination*, New York: Oxford University Press.

Spence, L. (2010) 'White space, black space', *The Urbanite*, 68: 43–45.

Turner, V. (1969) *The Ritual Process: Structure and Anti-Structure*, New York: New York University Press.

7

BLENDED LEARNING AND DATA
VERBALIZATION

This chapter suggests that data verbalization maybe used as a complimentary aid to progressing 'blended learning' located within a community context. I do not seek to replace other forms and approaches to learning but posit that in today's pressurized world of lecturing in higher education, there are a plethora of approaches, strategies, and ways of delivering learning, a blended approach is just one such option. I contend that 'data verbalization' can be a complimentary feature that could greatly assist an innovative approach to learning, when operating within communities who do not have full access to technological resources that forms the basis of blended learning. Blended learning is a pedagogical approach in which direct instruction moves from the group learning space to the individual learning space, and the resulting group space is transformed into a dynamic, interactive learning environment where the educator guides students as they apply concepts and engage creatively in the subject matter (Garrison & Vaughan, 2008). Traditionally, blended learning also involves using digital technology, such as video, to provide direct instruction on new concepts outside of the classroom. As students come to lessons with a preliminary understanding of the topic, this frees up class time for the teacher to focus on other beneficial learning activities. Students can then use lessons to build their understanding through discussion, collaborative activities and more practice. It can lead to students moving through content at their own pace, covering more, and in greater depth. It also fosters independent learning skills, making students aware of how they move through material, what they find difficult and what they excel at. I want to explore how an adapted form of blended learning can complement informal approaches to learning within a community setting. After presenting a paper at an international symposium (race matters) centring on race and crime scholarship, eminent African American professor (Penn State University) in an email referred to me as the 'epitome of an activist scholar'. He went further by encouraging me to continue to combine my passion for both research and social justice. As his comment settled into my sub-conscious I reflec-ted on how I had arrived at this juncture in my career. Throughout most of my academic career I have struggled on many levels with the burden of expectations placed upon my academic expertise. Flood, Martin, & Dreher (2013) cite dis-ciplinary and epistemological expectations placed on activist-scholars that at times places restriction on innovative practice. It is an experience I know only too well. On the one hand, I have always been told I must be innovative and creative in the classroom, but on the other, told my out-the-box thinking grates against the institution's ethos. I am similarly told that my academic input must gain peer reviewed validation knowing where issues of race are rendered invisible through the lens of 'disciplinary amnesia'.

The scholar–activist emerges

In 2015, I was disillusioned and angry at the constant battles I was having with col-leagues trying to dissuade me from pursuing my activist–scholar role. Needless to say, I ended up in a recording studio with community people who were more attentive to my work than my students. Most of those in the studio were young, black, and male. Many of them came from difficult backgrounds, had been in trou-ble with the law, and had disconnected from the social structure. After several weeks of informally engaging them with adapted mock lectures, it was evident that what was taken place was the evolution of a learning space that was community orien-tated. To my surprise a local university (not my own) heard about what was taking place and urged me to develop some bespoke lectures and run them formally. So, both myself and close friend, music producer Richard Campbell, transformed the studio into a working classroom. To support the learning we introduced live per-formances, food, and a physical environment of bean bags, settees, and chairs. The result transformed my whole way of being with relation to learning. The sessions ran over a period of time, sold out, alongside attracting disconnected and reluctant learners. It was a huge success. However, this small input pushed us to consider something much bigger in terms of community-based learning. Over the next few months both Richard and I laid the plans for creating our own centre dedicated to community and participatory learning. In 2017, we launched the BLESST centre (Building, Learning, Education, Safe, Space, Transition).

BLESST

The centre has the following key aims:

1.   BLESST is dedicated to creating an environment where there are opportu-nities for self-development, learning and transitional change for all commu-nity members.
2.   BLESST offers recreational and educational learning for people who are or have not had success in the pathways to accessing higher education.

3. BLESST aims to change the environment from a non-traditional space to a setting that is relative with fewer restrictions and boundaries to the learning process so that the experience can enhance the individual's chances to learn in a safe and transformative way.

From its inception, we ran small courses, workshops, and training sessions. By this time, I had found myself significantly involved in teaching on the Black Studies degree programme at Birmingham City University. Embedded into the black studies ethos was critical and radical pedagogy that would contest and challenge the dominance of white privileged notions of what constituted learning. In further conversations with attendees at the BLESST centre, black studies students, and a variety of community sources, it was clearly evident that there was a demand to bring the kind of academic education I was providing at my institution into the BLESST centre. The convergence of my work around 'data verbalization' could not have been timelier, as both Richard and I wanted to introduce the method into the learning at the BLESST centre. However, we both realized that if we set out to deliver teaching that was participatory and 'blended' we had to also find a community centred approach, as we didn't have the technological resources available. After some initial teething problems, we found a way through it. For those of you wanting to combine scholar–activism and community-centred blended learning, we hope that this chapter creates the possibility for you to move your learning outside of the academy.

Face the fear

With the introduction of more and more assessment measures for lecturers, the continuing push toward integrating higher education attainment with relation to employment, combined with the flux of differing and competing approaches to learning, it is clear that things in higher education are going through a pedagogical 'rite of passage'. To meet the challenges of these changes and to cater for the wide-ranging expectations of contemporary students there is a need to adopt and explore new paths to push educational opportunities for all, while at the same developing new modes of knowledge transfer. Even though I'm old school and prefer the human touch to the learning process, I am also a realistic and recognize the importance of managing my expectations within this current technological era. As a communicator of my ideas, who I am matters. The interaction, discussion, bringing creative techniques such as storytelling and drama into the classroom, are equally important as the students time away from the pressure of the classroom environment. In doing so I can also import much-needed social skills: cooperation, sharing, expression, and respecting other's views. I learned a great maxim from an elder: 'the elders are our textbooks'. Students learn not only from books, or from teachers teaching inside classroom but also from the co-students, through their peer group interaction, they learn many skills in playground and their small social interactions in canteens, lounge etc. When faced with having to consider traditional approaches to blended learning I was resistant, awkward, and if I'm being honest, scared. As someone who prided himself in the art of 'face-to-face' communication and student interaction, I was intimidated by the prospect of technology being deployed to do the job for me. However, in dialoguing with students I was made aware that 'blended' approaches are not an end in themselves but designed more to engage the student with a process of 'self-discovery' outside of the classroom. What I was reliably informed is that it was the actualization of bad 'blended learning' that was to blame. Further discussion with students enabled me to identify some of the additional concerns they had that would inform my own approach using 'data verbalization' in a blended learning context. I also recognized that in order to break any rules, one must know the previous rules as they existed before the desire to subvert or invert them.

- Participants who listened to several data verbalization tracks prior to any learning session within BLESST came with many of their own ideas that were triggered by the fusion of research and music. Important here what that in the face-to-face interactions student's felt that they engaged with the content easier when the musical input reflected their own tastes in music. Again, knowing your audience is important in this blended context. Using data verbalization in such a mediated context (screens and headphones) provided students with interaction of the workshop content in a versatile and unique way.
- The use of music on both audio and visual mediums meant that students were provided with an immersive experience to aid their learning. Interestingly, group discussion and exchange of ideas took place outside of the learning space; social media platforms, informally in alternative social spaces such as coffee houses, prior to coming into the workshop session provided an iterative experience where students had listened and discussed the data verbalization content many times, enabling to revise and edit their thinking in preparation for a wider discussion with their peers. This helped to build new confidences in the students, remove their hesitation and develop the skill of communicating effectively alongside enhancing their listening skills. By accessing data verbalization through screens and headphones students could learn anywhere, anytime and from anyone. Students became part of a mobile digital classroom irrespective of the geographical boundaries.

Intersectional blessings

A blended learning environment should be an intersection of personal interaction with lecturer and their classmates, alongside engaging with technological ways to engage with the course or module content. This in my view requires the lecturer to embrace, not reject the possibility of enhancing the learning experience. Early in my journey as a lecturer I did see myself as a so called 'expert' on my subject, not the enabler of joint and co-constructed ideas. I'd forgotten how much my students were versed in technology and knew more about its applications in ways that I was sadly lacking. Eventually, I saw a route through my ignorance. Basically, I involved my students in the design of my materials. Many of us feel that the only place learning takes place is in the classroom, where students sit and listen intently to what we say. However, recent experiences of engaging with student's distress confronted me with several other considerations that pushed me to reevaluate my learning approaches:

1. Some students are very social awkward and function better outside of the classroom. Of course, it would be great if every student were to feel safe alongside their peers. However, for students who suffer from anxieties, illness, or are generally isolated, the need to find new and improved ways for them to experiencing the positive benefits of learning was, and still is important. Many students have confided in me saying that they have friends and family outside of the university setting that at times help them engage in a more intimate way, given the right materials to work with. I have also been asked at times for one-to-one tutorials on mediums such as Skype, podcasts, and YouTube. Again, each one of those requests raised more questions.

2. As stated previously I am old school. I love to read, write, and engage in a dynamic classroom environment. However, I have also spent over three decades working in prisons where the deprivation of liberty sometimes means being held up in a classroom or confined space as part of a rehabilitative process. One thing I learned from working with offenders in prison settings, is the building of trust, when setting tasks for them to complete outside of the prison regime. In prison there are many competing interests that places massive restriction of the time of both the prison learner and the educator. Many times, when there was an issue with time, prison learners would have to go back to their cells to complete a task, and return equipped with responses to feed in to a wider group discussion. A frequent complaint for the critics of 'blended learning' is that students engage with the technology to learn, but at times avoid the classroom interaction. Therefore, central to my work on blended learning is to build mutual trust and respect for the process, not just to focus on the outcomes. Central to this proposition is placing important emphasis on the contribution of the prison learner outside of the classroom. Again, trust building with my students is based less on me testing what they have learned and more about the retention of their attendance throughout the lecturing period.

3. Learning that also imparts life skills have also been important to be. They are also important ingredients that employers look for, as well as equipping the individual with skills such as empathy, decision making capability, love, patience, communication, self-management, and critical thinking. To do this requires creating space for 'reflection'. At times the amount of information we have to process, share, and impart, makes it impossible to incorporate values within the learning process. As a child growing up my parents at a time of conflict would order me to go away and thing about things, and then return with any learning. At the time I could really see the value of their orders as I related it to punishment, not learning. However, there are many informal

encounters I have had with students who didn't manage to get listened to in the formal lecture or seminar, who wanted something clarified. It would usually result in recapping on what we'd be sharing, followed by some additional critical thoughts that would usually assist the student in going away and doing some of their own research to feed into the following week's discussion. Again, this informal aspect of my lecturing has featured much more formally, as it helps connect me to the students, and the student to the learning. In prison, they were called 'dialogue groups' and in a university setting 'communities of practice'. To my surprise students became more mindful, thoughtful, and overall more critical around subject matter they had felt excluded from or didn't understand.

4. There are times when the physical environment in a classroom is restrictive and punishing. When I am on a train, sitting in a theatre, or lounging around at home, the physical space we occupy assist us on so many different levels. Again, the amount of times students have asked me if they can sit on the floor, move around, or reposition the environment. The blended learning overcomes this limitation. Namely, because the interaction could be with a screen, a pair of headphones, a piece of music, all stimuli that enables the learner to incorporate some physical response to the content of the learning itself. For instance, beats make the feet move, a bassline can enable you to nod, a controversial clip may result in talking back to the screen, a powerful image or cluster of words can have a profound emotional impact. All of the previously mentioned activities can create an immense amount of fun, enjoyment, and complimentary stimuli for the learner. More importantly we should be involved in how our learners construct their own knowledge

Using 'data verbalization' as an adapted form of blended learning requires effective preparation. Researcher as educator involved in working with 'data verbalization' should be well acquainted with the concepts associated with both blended learning and be sufficiently skilled in creating and producing 'data verbalization'. They should be able to produce relevant content in a digital form in line with the way 'data verbalization' is produced. When co-producing data verbalization researchers should be prepared to share power within the process to bring confidence to participants. This in my view cements the co-constructed relationship between the researcher as educator and learner right from the outset. The beauty of data verbalization is that it does not require a significant IT set up unlike blended learning situations operating in universities and schools. Data verbalization can be accessed via social media platforms and piped into smartphones through headphones. Creating learning this way makes the experience truly 'democratic' and 'participatory'. Learners can also connect to each other via their own social network groups, talking and sharing ideas prior to engaging in the learning space. Important here is that the learning and sharing can also take place in virtual spaces such as Skype. In doing so, the learning is no longer restricted to a classroom, but a mediated space which can shared around the world. Again, the possibilities are endless, not limited to fixed spaces, or institutional governance. Indeed, an experience where 'data verbalization' was shared with a supervized activity in US prison as part of a home detention activity for pre-release prisoners was a case-in-point. The soon to be released prisoners would have access to my materials via 'data verbalization'. At an allotted time, I was then Skyped in, where a discussion ensued that aided the discussions regarding their reentry aspirations. Although blended learning has become well established in higher education 'data verbalization' has not yet been part of an expanding repertoire of digitized learning. I would like to suggest that data verbalization as an addition to blended learning can add value in the following areas:

- Community learners can be actively engaged in learning that is not institutionally based.
- Community learners can comprise individuals across the generations.
- Data verbalization can be part of a strategy to compensate for individuals who are not fortunate enough to go to a university.
- Data verbalization as a method can create enriching engagement possibilities that are community driven.
- Community learners using data verbalization as a method can access 'learning on the go' through headphones, making it a portable learning experience.
- Using data verbalization as part of a community-led blended learning strategy it can become a powerful for community transformation. It can also enable the researcher educator to co-produce more independent learning, with community members working at their own pace at home. The approach further enables community members to direct their own learning rather than relying on the researcher educator.

Case example: ode to Rosa

It was coming up to the Christmas period when student attendance is quite low, the weather posed logistical challenges, and I had reached the later part of the module. In my experience students at times will look at all of the on-line resources available and select which lectures/seminars they should attend. At the time of the assessment, some students do quite well by non-attendance, on-line reading, combined with 'leeching' off other students. It my view this highlights a consistent flaw within higher education. Namely, students can learn, pass their assessment, but never engage in a critical conversation about what they have learned. I was introducing the concept of desistance from crime, towards the end of the module. I was concerned that something that is important in the study of crime would be missed by students who had several other assignments to do. Luckily for me I had just created a 'data verbalization' story to jazz-hip hop about desistance. I encouraged students to download the track, and for those who didn't have access to downloading to enlist the support of other students. Overall, the track lasted no more than ten minutes, could be listened to via headphones or accessed via YouTube, and was presented in the vernacular that students could relate to. In the final recap session students returned to the class not only with critical thoughts about the content, but numerous suggestions about how to improve the method to aid their learning. Suddenly, we had gone from 'blended learning' at home, to 'learning on the go' where ever you were at the time. Students informed me that they had listened to the track at the gym, on the bus, in bed, and numerous other locations. In essence the learning took place when and where they wanted it to be. Plus, the knock-on effect: it provided a wider talking point in their social circles. What 'data verbalization' had succeeded in doing was to transcend the original designation of 'blended learning' and embed it into the student's socialization. Equally as important was the impact on colleagues who began to open a dialogue with myself regarding 'data verbalization' as a method of blended learning activity.

Abstract

Desistance from crime has been a considerable success story for academic criminology. The concept has deep roots, but did not emerge as a mainstream focus of study for the field until the 1990s movement toward developmental or life course criminology. From these origins, however, the term has taken on a life of its own, influencing policy and practice in criminal justice. This paper will briefly review this history, then explore what might be next for desistance research among numerous possible futures. I argue that the most fruitful approach would be to begin to frame and understand desistance not just as an individual process or journey, but rather as a social movement, like the civil rights movement or the 'recovery movements' among individuals overcoming addiction or mental health challenges. This new lens better highlights the structural obstacles inherent in the desistance process and the macro-social changes necessary to successfully create a 'desistance-informed' future.

Maruna, S. (2017) Desistance as a social movement, Irish Probation Journal, *(14): 5–20*

Ode to Rosa: desistance as a social movement

How do offenders reform themselves, reconnect to the social structure 'N' stay 'crime free'?

How does the *'counter narrative'* of those same reformed offenders hold the solution 'N' the key?

Where those returning from prison can return back to their families 'N' home communities

Where they can be part of processes and practices exploring mutual benefits 'N' real opportunities

At the heart of desistance is a very simple idea, namely, people can change, grow 'N' transform

In essence returning offenders can go through a *'rite of passage'*, start again, 'N' become reborn

This next chapter of the desistance story should be written by reformed offenders themselves

Where restrictions blocking their progression, should be locked in cupboards 'N' placed on shelves

Desistance from crime has been impacting 'N' effective 'N' has now clearly '*come of age*'

Influencing policy 'N' practice in the criminal justice system, on every level 'N' at every stage

Desistance now needs to become a *social movement* similar to both civil 'N' human rights

The focus on individual journeys, not programme outcomes, should firmly be set in its sights

Locating itself within the self-narratives of individuals who have moved away from crime

Showing how support 'N' guidance, can demonstrate how those individuals can change over time

It's not about '*what works*', but '*how it works*' 'N' what is beneficial 'N' mutually effective

It's time expose 'N' cast out biased assumptions that are oppressive, defunct, 'N' defective

It should focus less individual deficits, recognizing their individual strengths, talents, 'N' gifts

Designing interventions that provide opportunities for them not to stray, drop off, or jus' drift

It's not about fixing the offender, with experimental treatments, generating 'N' sustaining control

It's about developing meaningful relationships with meaningful support as a primary goal

Most people we label as '*offenders*' spend only a short time in their lives involved in criminality

Coz' if the cycle of offending isn't broken, the result is stagnation, distress 'N' further liminality

Building social capital 'N' improving personal strengths, should enable them to become reformed

However, there are structural obstacles in the way that blocks many from being '*desistance-informed*'

Studies of offenders over time demonstrates that most engage in criminal behaviours in their youth

Almost all of them 'grow out' of such things as they age, that's the evidence 'N' that's the proof

Scholars must now seek to understand, explain, research, how 'N' why individuals are able to desist

If not, the stories 'N' voices of the reformed offender will remain hidden, left out, 'N' surely missed

Be they former prisoners, reformed offenders, they can act as advocates, healers that are wounded

Their experiences can help others avoid their mistakes, part of the solution, included, not excluded

Sharing '*success stories*' of how they moved away from committing 'N' engagement with their crimes

These wounded healers could deliver the desistance message how people can change over time

They should be at the vanguard of *reintegration work* where it can have a direct and lasting impact

Their expertise, insights 'N' experiences, should be resourced, supported, 'N' more importantly backed

They should not be seen as the next *passing trend* or yet another exclusive 'N' intellectual fad

Where, the cry 'more research is needed' is merely an overused academic cliché that is merely bad

This evolution 'N' wounded healer revolution will be the emergence of desistance as a social movement

Where the voices, counter-narratives, 'N' lived experiences will lead to enrichment 'N' improvement

Which will take criminal justice agencies, academia, communities 'N' society in important new directions

Causing scholars 'N' agencies, to take on board the recommendations of wounded healer reflections

Similar social movements have transformed the fields of mental health, dementia 'N' addiction

Where stigmatized groups have collectively organized for their rights 'N' accurate depiction

Removing the ownership 'N' control from the Ivory Tower, the world of probation, 'N' prisons,

Back to the communities where desistance takes place 'N' 'wounded healers' take the active decisions

In collaboration 'N' partnership, co-produced by activists, agents of change 'N' grassroots organisation

Drawing on convict criminologists themselves presented through inclusive community dissemination

Providing a supportive community 'N' a network of individuals with common 'N' shared experiences

Free from control agents intervention, or academia's biased assumptions 'N' restrictive inferences

These groups will draw attention to the macro-political issues involved in crime, justice and reintegration

Challenge the myths, 'N' develop a frame of reference that moves from despair to emancipation

The primary challenge that ex-prisoners face in reintegrating into society is they are hugely stigmatized

Although each person manages stigma differently, it is experienced collectively where most are victimized

Stigmatized groups should be involved in advocacy 'N' speaking out that is human 'N' self-enhancing

Whilst effectiveness by such participation helps to restore self-esteem without sideways glancing

Wounded healers can become involved in giving meaning, purpose, social 'N' cultural significance

To a formerly incarcerated person's life, motivate, inspire, transform, 'N' make a real difference

Traditional research practices will inevitably have to adapt to remain true to the desistance idea

Research endeavours will need to become more inclusive, 'N' not driven by suspicion 'N' fear

Involving wounded healers themselves in gathering data, analysis 'N' collective interpretation.

With a maxim that *nothing about us without us,* means inclusive 'N' meaningful participation

If experts want to convene a conference the voices of the wounded healer must be profiled 'N' heard

'N' represented in policy discussions, so the stories of their lives are not rendered invisible 'N' blurred

There is a need to understand the stories of communities that are impacted by flawed 'N' biased policies

Where the inclusion of such voices leads to progress without fear, contradiction, or apologies

There should be no processes where there is othering, bigotry, implicit bias 'N' de-humanization

That restricts meaningful dialogue, blocks progressive leadership 'N' inhibits communication

Far from undermining conducting research, criminological teaching, scholarship 'N' theorising

Such developments should breathe new life into the classroom, making research more enterprising

Making criminology more relevant, up-to-date and as an academic area of study 'N' investigation

That is, inclusive social science is *good* social science, should be embraced without any hesitation

How do offenders reform themselves, reconnect to the social structure 'N' stay 'crime free'?

How does the 'counter narrative' of those same offenders hold both the solution 'N' the key?

Where those returning from prison can be reincorporated back in their home communities

Where everyone is brought together to explore mutual benefits 'N' real opportunities

Desistance from crime has been a considerable success story 'N' has now come of age

Influencing policy 'N' practice in criminal justice, on every level 'N' at every stage

The focus on individual journeys, not programme outcomes, should firmly be set in its sights

Desistance now needs to become a social movement similar to that of civil 'N' human rights

At the heart of desistance is a very simple idea, people can change, grow 'N' transform

In essence offenders can go through a '*new rite of passage*', start again, 'N' become reborn

Conclusion

As discussed blended learning can be engaging and 'fun' for students, as a result of it being a new and fresh approach and a change from traditional teaching approaches that use technology less frequently. In turn, students' increased enjoyment of using this approach can positively impact on their attitudes toward learning as a whole. Whereas the blended classroom model is very dependent on technology; students must have access to a computer (or similar device) and the internet so they can watch videos at home, 'data verbalization' can be accessed simply by subscribing to social media plat-forms on tablets and smartphones. Similar to blending a classroom, data verbalization requires considerable time and commitment in its planning. However, with the infu-sion of music, rhymes, and strong spoken narrative, the preparation presented in a way that connects to the listener will be profitable in many ways. Leaners who connect emotionally to the content; music and words, will engage based on having a sensory experience. The key ingredient here is knowing your audience. Unlike schools and universities who have a rigid and fixed curriculum, researcher educators can set their own agenda based on an evidence-based need. The key element here is in the researcher educators ability to create 'data verbalization' stories that capture the ima-gination, incorporate the learning, and engage at both the emotional and intellectual level. Whereas the success of the blended classroom is very dependent on video quality (Bergmann, 2016 Bergmann & Sams, 2012); data verbalization must be recorded well. With high quality audio recording equipment being made available it is an accessible and cost-effective way to produce content as laid out in Chapter Four. Overall, 'data verbalization' offers numerous possibilities to engage learners in distinct ways free from the clutter of the fixed terrain of traditional settings.

Summary

This chapter looked at the way data verbalization can be used as a complimentary approach with relation to blended learning. It also examined ways to look beyond the traditional approaches to blended learning by examining possible new concepts out-side of the classroom. This chapter concluded by exploring the consequences and implications of deploying such as approach for student learning.

Reflection questions

1.   What are the triumphs and tensions using a blended learning approach within your own research?
2.   How do you envision using new approaches to students learning using your research?

References

Bergmann, J. (2016) Flipped classroom approach. *World Journal on Educational Technology*, 8: 98–105.
Bergmann, J. & Sams, A. (2012) *Flip Your Classroom: Reach Every Student in Every Class Every Day*. Oregon: International Society for Technology in Education.
Flood, M., Martin, B. & Dreher, T. (2013) Combining academia and activism: Common obstacles and useful tool, *Australian Universities Review*, 55(1): 17–26.
Garrison, D.R. & Vaughan, N. (2008) *Blended Learning in Higher Education: Framework, Principles, and Guidelines*. San Fransisco, CA: Jossey-Bass.
Maruna, S. (2017) Desistance as a social movement, *Irish Probation Journal*, 14: 5–20.

8

DATA VERBALIZATION AND SOCIAL MEDIA

This reflexive chapter is unapologetically subjective. It is not designed to give a critique of the technological nuances of 'social media', nor is it designed to argue the merits of social media as a global phenomenon. This chapter therefore positions itself with relation to the dominant and exclusive peer review system that excludes 'out-the-box thinking' for academic renderings that are situated based on a set format that seldom accommodates differing ways of exploring academic ideas. On-line publishing does not equate to more 'digitized forms' of looking at data other than journal articles. I am not pleading for a special case or expressing outrage for this state of affairs. The call to arms here is less about seeking approval from my peers, and centres purely on how 'data verbalization' can play an active role in assisting activist researchers whose work is seen as risky, contentious, or doesn't sit right within the neo-liberal definitions of what constitutes 'real' research.

Race Matters Symposium

In 2018, I attended an international symposium at the London School of Economics. This event was convened because of the concerns that despite the continuing recognition of the over-representation of black and minority ethnic men and women in criminal justice interventions, empirical research in the criminal justice field that focuses on race, remains scarce and mainstream criminological scholarship is theoretically under-developed with regard to race. The overarching theme was the urgent need to kick-start a new dialogue that connected the sociological theorization of race/ethnicity with the increasingly marginalized position of race within criminological scholarship. An amazing array of speakers was lined up, myself included. Most presentations were informative, insightful, and at times challenging. I decided that it was appropriate to focus less on what we research, and to address how we get our messages across. Previous speakers had focussed on how my discipline of criminology operated with a 'colour blind' approach, frequently operated with 'unconscious bias', and lacked visual recognition of the contribution of both race and race scholars to the study of crime. This for me felt less about the need to do more research, and more of the need to get what existed out there into the wider public domain. Indeed, it was opening point in my presentation that if researchers are to become part of a wider dialogue with relation to social justice, then maybe we need to rethink who our audience is for our work. Is it peer review journals, academic silos, restrictive funding bodies, or are there new alliances to forge? I called for a revolution in how race scholarship is disseminated, and to further consider new and improved ways to locate research outside of the academy. Some scholars argue that no one method can adequately lay claim to holding the answers of the complex nature of how race centred research can impact on areas such as the criminal justice system. It is therefore incumbent for all researchers to transcend straightforward explanations and neat theoretical under-standings and occupy space outside of the comfort zone of the 'ivory tower'. Instead I feel a move toward a moment that moves toward a more 'mediated imagination' is now required. So, I proceeded with my presentation using 'data verbalization' as my *modus operandi*. After finishing my presentation, you could have heard a pin drop. The silence was piercing. No-one had heard anything like it. The subtext of what I'd done was contained in awkward body language, sighs and gasps, alongside sheer shock at what had taken place. I concluded my presentation by stating clearly that by using 'data verbalization' this way I had found a way of sharing complex ideas in an accessible, potent, and impactful way. If I ever felt edgy about whether or not my peers would embrace 'data verbalization', I underestimated the power of what I'd done, alongside realizing that on the continuum of dissemination I had just extended the boundaries. Here I would like to borrow from science fiction as a metaphor for the path that I was now on. There is now the proliferation of on-line blogging, high performance phone cameras with easy access to digital platforms. However, there are other debates that need to be had, new concerns that need to be raised and con-temporary understandings that must be posited. It is to those sceptics, critics, and detractors I offer this chapter. For those who like me are sick of having to defend our researcher identity for fear of retribution from those who feel an existential threat. I hope you find some comfort in this small offering.

Context

When I first encountered social media, I had a massively tough time. I didn't know where I fitted in, how to operate on any of the platforms, and many other levels of anxiety governed my disdain for the medium. It was in the development of 'data verbalization' that confronted me with my short comings and failure to grasp the importance of how I could disseminate my work in ways that would 'reach' and 'impact' on a scale I had not foreseen. I can't remember where it was, but I read an article on social media and discovered a new word to add to my impoverished understanding that brought a smile to my face. That word was 'disintermediation', which essentially meant 'getting rid of the middleman'. It was music to my ears. It meant I could name what I wanted 'data verbalization' to become. I wanted something that could go straight to the consumer. Examples of 'disintermediation' are those people who can book their own air flights and holidays instead of using travel agents; ordering cars online; and products that can be bought direct from manufacturers. This is my view has given 'data verbalization' a strong 'democratic edge'. Rogers (2009) argues that data collection could benefit from thinking about how on-line techniques can be repurposed for research dissemination. Rogers further calls for a new era in researching on-line, which does not concern itself with the divide between the 'real' and 'the virtual'.

Measurement issues

The issue should focus less on measuring the quantitative elements of on-line consumption and more on how to herald an era that brings cultural change and societal shifts using social media. Bruns (2015) points out that the processes of media production are social processes just as much as the activities of media audiencing. Bruns (2015) continues by arguing that all media are social media, operating on a networked, many-to-many, rather than a broadcast, one-to-many basis. Bruns understands that social media is by default inclusive rather than elite, with the means of media production in the hands of the people free from editorial control. Langlois (2015) also sees the rise of social media platforms, combined with the shift in knowledge and economic production toward big data, has fundamentally transformed the stakes of critical research, that is, research that identifies power inequalities to develop alternatives. More generally, we now face the growing impossibility of doing independent critical research because research into the social has now become a closed market. It has yet to be seen or tested with relation to how 'data verbalization' can operate on social media platforms free from intervention. Increasingly as the public becomes the arbiters of taste regarding social media, more research needs to be undertaken to project some long term thinking into the pitfalls that may emerge. Where does 'data verbalization' on social media fit in the research world? As researchers adopt new methods such as 'data verbalization' more investigation needs to take place in the way researcher's present new ways of communicating their work. Given the particular nuances and requirements of the modern-day research environment, I argue that social media meets dissemination needs in very different ways. But being aware of these specific needs for your own research project will help you decide where to invest your energies and what types of digital content may be worth experimenting with.

Considerations

Before undertaking a data verbalization project on social media, it is essential that you take the time to consider some key questions over what you want out of your project and the audiences you intend to reach. This will not only allow you to reflect critically on the means by which you will disseminate your content, but also allow you to address any potential barriers before they risk becoming a hindrance later on. Why do you want to put data verbalization on social media? Is it because you want to reach influencers like journalists or special interest groups? Or do you simply want to raise awareness among a more general audience? Consider whether data verbalization you intend to produce gather has the potential to do this, and whether your audience will be interested enough to engage with it. When thinking about how you might disseminate your research using photos or videos on social media, explore what specific stories you can tell. As you are sharing your content on social media, you need a punchy, clear delivery. Think of a story in the classic sense here: exposition, rising action, climax, falling action and resolution. If you are using data verbalization as part of the dissemination and impact phases of the research lifecycle, you should already be considering who your audiences might be and what expectations they might have. Audiences and the actions you want your audiences to take will influence the style of the content you produce and how you use social media to promote it.

Podcasting

A good fit for 'data verbalization' is using the method to generate an interesting 'podcast' format. Podcasts from academic and research organisations though dominated by the standard lecture are becoming increasingly varied as universities and funding bodies invest more in diverse forms of dissemination in order to react to audience trends and interests. Increased social media and digital engagement can help grow your audiences beyond the confines of academic journals and those research communities already plugged into the literature. Likewise, podcasting puts your research on a completely new platform, increasing the odds that new audiences from politicians to the lay persons will hear about your research. Researchers looking to reach wider audiences outside of those already in tune to the usual ivory tower publishing channels can do so through podcasting. Podcasting is also useful as a tool throughout the research lifecycle. The audio-based medium also presents a means to distinguish yourself from the crowded and competitive research landscape. At the same time, it is an accessible and easy means of achieving all these ends. So how do lecturers move beyond the confines of traditional approaches to teaching and lecturing at a time when the wider pedagogical expectations are now firmly located within the Teaching in Excellence Framework (TEF)? Are new teaching and assessment tools now required? I am calling for the creation and development of a 'participatory learning spaces' where the intersection of 'theory', 'praxis', and 'reflexivity' among both students and lectures can coexist alongside each other in community spaces. To do so requires a move towards a 'participatory pedagogy'.

Participatory Pedagogy

Participatory Pedagogy (PP) can be defined as 'methods and practices to empower students to present, share, analyse and to reflect on their learning, as the basis of 'enhancing both social capital and action'. I come to this position based on recent experiences over the last couple of years where I have observed a negative shift in the overall participation, mood, and engagement of my students. Levels of anxiety, despondency, and at times disconnectedness from the overall learning experience have been clearly visible. The outcomes have also at times resulted in poor attendance, a lack of overall attainment, combined with a reduction in 'employability skills' required to locate students' aspirations within the wider social structure. The evaluation of these experiences would suggest there is are significant problems going unaddressed which is deeply troubling. Of late I have undertaken several …

- … Identity and self-concept building workshops as part of BCU's Graduate plus week, as well as students from other faculties;
- … community-based learning workshops in a variety of settings;
- … prison-based learning sessions.

Reflecting on these current situations I have become even more convinced of the need to enhance my connection with my students: to cross boundaries of participation, with a view to increasing their academic attainment, confidence, and employability. Therefore, the need to create a 'safer and more transformative space' has now become significant to make the learning experience for both myself and my students even more open and democratic. It is also my view that it may be time to reassess not just 'what' is taught in my classroom/s, but 'how' things are taught. Recent developments such as 'blended' and 'flipped' learning have created significant new possibilities for recalibrating pedagogical expectations across the teaching of many disciplines as a whole. However, surveying some of the literature surrounding pedagogies there is an absence of a more diverse, creative, and innovative approaches to delivering 'participatory pedagogy' using social media approaches with methods such as 'data verbalization'. Disseminating your findings gives your research on social media can give a much greater impact, help to inform the wider public about policy issues and has the potential to change lives and communities for the better if the awareness can be raised triggering 'praxis'. It should then allow other communities and groups to make their own choices regarding social action more efficient and effective because the sharing and learning has been accessible, open, and transparent. It has never been easier to get your message out to the people and organizations who can benefit from your work than using social media and data verbalization.

Social media and you

Firstly, let me say that I am not a great fan of social media with relation to the personal side of things. Overall, I have found it to be intrusive, impersonal, and unfriendly. However, in relation to research dissemination I have found t to be of significant use. In order for me to benefit from the various platforms without becoming obsessed I developed the following strategy that might be of some help:

1. **Delegation:** Surrounding myself by individuals who were savvy and up to speed with the latest developments, sites, and insights, enabled me to delegate some of the needs I had. In doing so it was less stressful, plus I was in a position to draw on the strengths of those in the know, this increasing my own awareness.
2. **Tutorials:** When faced with some of my own fears regarding social media I undertook several on-line tutorials to face some of my fears and strengthen my weaknesses.
3. **Books:** I decided to purchase a range of informative books on social media, not just to increase my knowledge, but to build a reservoir of information that could feed into my research. Again, in doing so my confidence has grown over time.
4. **Networks:** By putting my work onto various social media sites I have built up a significant following. By engaging with my constituents (followers) I have been exposed to a range of on-line communities who are supportive and share their insights and tips with me.
5. **Face the fear:** As I get older I find myself having to challenge myself by facing my fears. So rather than take myself seriously as if my life depends on it, I engage with social media as a way of confronting and beating any fears I might have.

There are no hard and fast rules with relation to engaging with social media. However, there are thousands of sites, acres of information, and many bespoke communities. So, all I can advise you to do is to experiment and connect to the on-line world.

Data verbalization on social media

This section details some of my current work on data verbalization available on the following social media platforms:

- Spotify
- Soundcloud
- iTunes
- Amazon
- Deezer
- YouTube

Breaking Free (2018) is a 'data verbalization' jazz hip-hop track based on the 'diary of a prostate sufferer' by Dr Martin Glynn. Adapted by Dr Martin Glynn. Produced by Natural and Secret (Birmingham).

Ode to Rosa: Desistance as a social movement (2018) is a 'data verbalization' jazz hip-hop track. Adapted from the article: 'Desistance as a social movement' (*Irish Probation Journal*, 2017) by Professor Shadd Maruna. Adapted by Dr Martin Glynn. Produced by Natural and Secret (Birmingham).

Silenced (2016) is a 'data verbalization' jazz hip-hop track. (Available of ITunes and Spotify.) Adapted from Glynn, M. (2016) 'Towards an intersectional model of desistance for black offenders', *Safer Communities*, 15(1): 24–32. Adapted and written by Dr Martin Glynn. Produced by Natural and Secret (Birmingham).

Article 51 (2016) is a 'data verbalization' jazz hip-hop album. (Available of ITunes, Spotify, and Amazon). Adapted from several of Dr Glynn's academic journal articles. Adapted and written by Dr Martin Glynn. Produced by Natural and Secret (Birmingham).

Summary

This chapter called for the dissolution of conventional understandings and accepted boundaries with relation to how research is disseminated, and to consider new and improved ways to locate research outside of the academy. It further argued that no one method can adequately lay claim to holding the answers of the complex nature of how research can impact in areas such as social and racial justice based on a lack of unification among academic disciplines. It concluded by calling for researchers to transcend straightforward explanations and neat theoretical understandings and occupy space outside of the comfort zone of the 'ivory tower'. Instead this is a historical moment that requires a move towards a more 'mediated imagination'.

Reflection questions

1. Where do sit in relation to a mediated imagination of your research?
2. What role do you feel social media should play in disseminating research?

References

Bruns, A. (2015) 'Making sense of society through social media', *Social Media + Society*, 1: 1–2.
Langlois, G. (2015) 'What are the stakes in doing critical research on social media platforms?' *Social Media + Society*, 1: 1–2.
Rogers, R. (2009) 'The End of the Virtual – Digital Methods', Text prepared for the Inaugural Speech, Chair, New Media & Digital Culture, University of Amsterdam.

EPILOGUE – FUTURE DIRECTIONS

Relief

The irony of the term epilogue in this context suggests the ending or conclusion of the book. In actuality this is just the start of a new journey of discovery. A journey where the first chapter has just been completed. Writing this book has proven to be challenging on many levels. Firstly, the content is less informed by its predecessors: applied theatre, ethno-drama, performance auto-ethnography, and more by the desire to create a blueprint for the next generation who are fully immersed in democratizing the way in which research disseminated. In doing so one of the greatest challenges was to provide a text that satisfied some the academic in me, but more importantly spoke to the artist in the academic. It is now my desire to see 'data verbalization' being located at the forefront of research dissemination heralding a new era with relation to the distribution of research data as a whole.

Pressing need

As I have argued throughout, there is a pressing need to represent 'critical research dissemination' as a counter-narrative function that contests, challenges, and exposes oppressive, dominant, and privileged research paradigms. My position might sound exclusionary (and therefore problematic), but I feel strongly that scholarship in the field of research dissemination within the academy is severely lacking because of the ways universities work to maintain the privilege of compliant scholars to the exclusion of scholars committed to social justice goals. For those researchers who are comfortable with the peer review system, satisfied with having their research side-lined as it's not 'impacting' enough, or followers of a system that excludes many different types of research/researcher, I am hoping to tempt you to at least consider the propositions laid out in this book. For those researchers who like me is tired, worn out, and demoralised by the lack of attention paid to their work, then maybe these final thoughts will incentivize you to continue to find, discover, and create ways of disseminating research that becomes part of a wider continuum within research as a whole. I also want to confront any detractors who dismiss my views as merely academic rants. I make no apology for being fuelled by a sense of academic injustice that privileges others based on bias and supremacy. To my critics I embrace the exclusion you have created, as it has pushed me to generate a legacy for my work that transcends the limited expectations that I have been exposed to for most of my academic life. Bell (2003) similarly calls for future research to move beyond mere descriptive accounts of social phenomena and sees the need to address how intersectional inequalities influence research outcomes for marginalized populations. Data verbalization as discussed in these few chapters is ideally placed to assist marginalized communities in bringing attention to their concerns by presenting research data creatively. Data verbalization does not stand alone in this endeavour as my discovery is part of a historical legacy of others who have trod the same path at different times in history, in search of new and improved ways to get research 'heard', 'seen' and 'experienced'. For me this position calls upon academics, artists, practitioners, and other related interests to form alliances and movements that will provide the impetus for validating approaches to research dissemination that works towards wider social/racial justice aims. The building of such alliances and movements should create opportunities to gain new insights and understandings through which to assess those factors and processes that would enhance marginalized communities' ability to improve their engagement with, and connection to, wider public and social policy concerns, while at the same time shaping how those policies are designed and delivered.

Academia and beyond

The need to share, disseminate, and present research data beyond academia is a key motivating factor in a world that increasingly needs to present its findings in ways that are culturally competent, accessible, and interactive. The significant outcomes generated during the development phase of 'data verbalization' would suggest that the deployment of performative method for disseminating and sharing research has now extended beyond its inception, creating extensive possibilities and a variety of new opportunities for presenting research data as a whole. Important here is data verbalization must not replicate a structure that oppresses and excludes, but instead create a more equitable and empowering way to function and live in a society that still privileges different groups over each other. The academic in me wants to change the structure, yet I know operating from a position of privilege is not helpful. Hence the need to reposition myself and relocate myself back into a community content. In essence bringing academia to the streets. Living with such a contradiction means I can no longer justify being in an academic environment that doesn't connect itself in some way to meaningful and relevant political, social, and cultural change that will make the world a better place to be. So, if the truth be told I'm still more like Malcolm 'X' than Martin Luther King. What I want deep down is more humanity and less punitive responses metered out to those who happen to fall outside the boundaries of what is perceived to be a fair society. With any actions come consequences. The consequences of not pursuing my passion will be more detrimental that accepting the comfort of apathy. I observe the helplessness of many people around me who are driven to despair as they lose hope. I also watch those around me breaking down as they have their hopes and dreams destroyed by holding on to a past that is painful, combined with never grieving over loss. It all mounts up and makes many of us crippled by emotional pain that is held captive by a system that fuels it, ensuring we remain held captive to negativity. The definitions and labels we apply to ourselves leave little room for personal growth, when those definitions remain fixed. I am a fluid human being who is still growing, still curious, still looking into new ways of being. However, if I am not open to new types of exploration then those who label me negatively will be the ultimate victors. So here I am wondering if my 'contribution to knowledge' will ever truly be seen, heard, or make me a household name or like many of my predecessors locate me within the confines of second hand bookshop shelves. I have therefore decided it is time to 'remove my mask', reclaim the context of my 'academic space' to reveal my 'own truth' and present my own 'counter narrative'. Emirbayer and Desmond (2012) point out that our understanding of the 'racial and social order' will remain forever unsatisfactory so long as we fail to turn our analytic gaze back upon ourselves and begin to inquire critically into the 'hidden' presuppositions that shape our thinking. They further call for critical reflexivity to be employed by researchers who must acknowledge that reflexive thinking entails much more than observing how one's social position affects our overall analysis. As stated previously, while the struggle for validating my 'insider' researchers position continues to throw up challenges, the impact of my academic 'invisibility' is made worse, when at times my research insights and understandings are still marginalized by those who operate from a so-called privileged epistemological vantage point.

The racialized researcher's burden

Rich (2009) when recounting his experiences on the stories of young black men who had experienced trauma as a consequence of street-based violence states, 'without any access to their voices, we could easily formulate solutions that are out of sync with the reality of their lives and that would be ineffective and downright destructive'. These accounts clearly make a point that demands to be discussed. The world at times is messy, dangerous, and chaotic and cannot always been measured objectively or quantified by assumptions that omit the lived reality of those being investigated. Denzin (2010) in his attempt to direct attention to the need to transcend the confines of the 'ivory tower' calls upon those scholars who believe in the connection between 'critical inquiry' and 'social justice'. Serrant-Green (2010) likewise calls for new frameworks to be developed when researching 'sensitive issues' or 'marginalized perspectives' from populations who have been 'pathologized' more than respected and understood within the research domain. It is my experience that many researchers undertaking so-called 'risky' research are excluded from research bids, never taken seriously by other academics who feel that 'objectivity', 'longitudinal studies', and abstract concepts, takes precedence over using research for an equally noble cause such as social justice. Several of my black academic friends have escaped from the confines of the inner city in favour of the sunnier climes of the US, in search of a bigger salary and improved status within the established African American academic fraternity.

Defiant

Tempting as it has been, I have not yet succumbed to the possibility of relocation, but the door is still open. A history of racial subordination has made me more vigilant and defiant in the face of continuing and sustainable pressure coming from forces designed to keep me and my work down. I've grown tired of having to seek permission, gain access, go through intermediaries, and negotiate with gatekeepers. I'm worn down by continually providing evidence only to have it replaced by bias and limited theories who claim some kind authentic right to judge my own views without challenge. How then does someone like me maintain the balance between challenging the status quo, while at the same time not get sucked into the very psychic machinery that tries grinds your energy down to nothing? My academic work centres on researching stuff that most don't take seriously, located within the pervasive 'sound bite culture', where nothing really comes out of it, except I can say I tried my best, answered a hypothesis, or at best I get invited to speak in public. The commitment for implementing the changes outlined in countless research inquires I've been involved in has at best become destined to be part of an academic fairy tale. The academic in me wants to change the structure, yet I know operating from that privileged position weakens my own position when working with disaffected people. Like many researchers I have had to constantly negotiate a devalued status that requires extensive 'emotion management'. I know only too well that progressive researchers and activist scholars function in different realities. Where racialization is concerned many white academics operate in a social space where 'whiteness' is privileged and thus taken for granted; while blackness is both discredited and devalued, unless notions of class are located as a refuge for neo-liberals to hide in the shadows of identity politics. It is my view that the binary of academic 'blackness' and 'whiteness' ultimately shapes the understanding, interpretation, and management of those experiences. This is combined with the weight of at times having to represent the entire black community which is both unrealistic and emotionally draining. For me participation in dominant white institutions requires black academics to exhibit extraordinary emotional restraint referred to as 'moderate blackness'.

Moderate blackness

Moderate blackness entails an approach to racial politics and the ability to get along with white people where notions of blackness become invisible. These strategies work together to produce restrained emotions and require black academics not to see or acknowledge oppressive racialized constructs. Moderate blackness in my view circumscribes the range of my emotional and political expression, constraining not just my feelings but the cognitive attention as well. It thus manages the individual problems I face in the academy but does not challenge the basis for the different emotional rules that constrain them in the first place. It also limits my ability to see or address other forms of race-based treatment that might constrain my future mobility. At times trying to occupy a 'race neutral' position has pushed me to breaking point resulting in some deep seated 'psychic resentment' at those who do not have to face the situations I face. When I refused to be 'invisible', I was slapped down, forced to compromise my integrity, and become part of a neo liberal agenda of 'identity politics'. This became very confusing and disconcerting at the best of times, as it made me believe that I was responsible for my own oppression and subsequent subordination. I am no Uncle Tom, nor am I a revolutionary with a single focus hell bent of destroying white society. However, for most of my life I have found myself constantly having to defend my own sense of 'racialized identity' as a 'black man', to both black and white people alike. This constant toing and froing of black and white people, (men in particular), using flawed 'identity politics' masquerading as 'pseudo race relations', has continuously attempted, but failed to disable my own sense of identity. A recent connection with Lester Spence, an African American professor at Johns Hopkins has helped me contextualize my own predicament as well as moving me beyond the realms of being boxed into a corner. Like me, Lester was tired of being defined by white people's expectations and decided to reframe his sense of 'self' and 'place', choosing to situate himself within the confines of Baltimore's black community. He revealed his need 'to have a space in which he did not have to defend his racial existence'. His humanity was borne out of a desire to just 'be', not to defend his difference to those who didn't share the same perspective. Not only do I share his view, I also refused to succumb to the will of others, who feel that 'assimilation' is good for the control of my soul. I like who I have become but am sick and tired of being around those 'energy draining' individuals whose insecurities, lack of identity, wander around aimlessly trying to impose their fragile elitist personas onto me, as subtly as a sledgehammer knocking a wall down. African American author James Baldwin when living in exile in France was forced to examine his sense of self. Similar to Baldwin my existence within academia (which at times felt like being in exile), forced me to examine how I live and function, alongside the changing nature of my relationship to the community where I reside. So, I refused to surrender my identity to those individuals who would seek to convince me otherwise for the sake of maintaining their privileged position over me. One explanation is that black researchers, qualified as we are, are rendered powerless in an academic system that privileges one group over the other, where policy responses, legislative changes, and other responses do not provide us with a sense of equal justice in terms of access to validating both our research and the methods we employ. How then do 'on road' researchers like me maintain the balance between challenging the status quo, while at the same time not being sucked in to the very machinery that grinds their energy down, forcing us away from researching that is meaningful and important? The inability of those black researchers who suffer racial disparities in the criminal justice research to successfully operate independently of street level bureaucrats, policy makers, and strategic agencies is also problematic and requires a new approach that provides a shared platform that has power to determine its own destiny.

Who knows it, feels it

Friere (1970) states

> who are better prepared than the oppressed to understand the terrible significance of an oppressive society? Who suffer the effects of oppression more than the oppressed? Who can better understand the necessity of liberation?
>
> *(1970: 27)*

Who better than Friere to articulate something is a reality for those of in and outside of the academy who are equally affected by oppression? Like Friere, a committed progressive researcher must be someone who acknowledges that liberation from oppressive forces must be a key goal when researching with communities who themselves are oppressed and require support in transforming pain and suffering into healing and transformation. It is my contention that residents of inner city communities who are exposed to extreme levels of poverty, crime, and violence in context are both the 'experts' and 'knower's' of their own experiences. In a world of binaries inner city communities are often portrayed as 'no go' zones, places to pass through, and not to live. Seldom is the resilience, cohesion, and strength of those who live under difficult circumstances acknowledged in an academic world that would rather create a nightmare scenario, than one of occupying a difficult space and thriving. The inner-city communities I'm referring to and am connected to have given the world so many positive things, which are seldom, explored in crime dramas, reality TV shows, or indeed academic journals. Much about what I've read about my reality paints a picture that not only distorts the reality but generates subtle forms of 'moral panic' that wants to create the world I live in as hedonistic, lawless, and no moral centre. The inner-city communities I visit and live among offer all criminologists an opportunity to engage in a dialogue around those same understandings, thoughts, feelings, insights, and experiences through telling their own stories and more importantly in their own words. My own story therefore highlights the important contribution of the communities I engage with, in playing a key role that informs our understanding of the social conditions that shapes and affects their lives, with specific reference research dissemination. This book also speaks to those excluded, marginalized, and neglected researchers, who like me, feel it is time for our voices to be heard, as well as exercising our right to contest the views of those who 'talk cricket from the boundary, but seldom face a fast bowler from the crease'.

The 'ebony tower'

As stated previously Dubois (1938) sees researchers who do not venture into inner city communities as 'carwash sociologists'. While Katz (1988) equally as condemning similarly criticises those social scientists who can 'graciously transport themselves' to worlds they have never been before by making claims from the 'safe vantage point' of the 'ivory tower'. The 'ebony tower' position is relevant here when it comes to research dissemination. The ebony tower is 'inclusive' not 'exclusive'. It starts from a position that acknowledges the limitations of the researcher can be strengthened by a community's engagement and involvement with the formulation, undertaking, and dissemination of research inquiries that will have impact on their lives. For some researchers the newly formed hypothesis and the accessing of the resources to undertake an inquiry will emerge 'post-event/s', when there is sufficient distance and reflection to warrant such an investigation. However, the need to make sense of the chaos in the 'eye of the storm' is also an important consideration in relation to insights that can be gained 'in the moment' the event occurs. Serrant-Green (2010) calls for new frameworks to be developed when researching sensitive issues or 'marginalized perspectives' from populations who have been 'over pathologized' within the so-called mainstream research domain. 'What happens when you can't get a research grant? When you have no tenure?' Or the 'insider perspective you hold is labelled too subjective, militant, or challenges the orthodoxy? What do you do when you are at times stigmatized on account of coming from the same community and have the cultural background as your research participants? Data verbalization's future vision therefore aims to locate the performative aspect of research within a global context, alongside its continual development through a laboratory process. In doing so it hoped to bring performed research data into space that moves beyond the confines of academia. Equally as important is to equip researchers, educators, practitioners, and other related professionals with the tools to turn research data into 'mobilized action' that will lead to wider environmental, social, and cultural impacts. It is befitting at this stage to add a few of my own thoughts about the wider issue of the key principles that should underpin all good research dissemination. Co-constructed and co-produced research dissemination should entail engaging with community members throughout the process from inception to conclusion. In order to do so the researcher must establish their credibility with their target audience and commit themselves to developing a meaningful and productive working relationship. Here I would like to draw on my experience as an ethnographer. Gaining access, building relationships, connecting to people, alongside sharing insights and knowledge takes times, commitment, and energy. However, done correctly the researcher then becomes an integral, not a dominant or controlling element within the wider community as a whole. As we have discussed universities and those vested interests who at times colonise the research landscape have created innovative ways to locate their messages through slick and powerful marketing campaigns. Research dissemination that will invariably impact on the lives of community members should aim to be presented in formats that are appropriate, relevant, and accessible. The key consideration here therefore is knowing ones audience. In my own work I am interested in ensuring that important insights, messages, and ideas locate themselves in the hearts and minds of those who need the changes to improve their lives. Overall, the building of partnerships with established networks will support the wider exchange of knowledge emerging from the researchers work. Communities who lack resources will at some stage need champions who themselves have influence and reach. In saying that those same partners should have a proven track record of operating with the same ethical principles as the researcher and target audience. Understanding the context of the research outcomes may also require influential opinion leaders on board to act as champions. In order to create an infrastructure to kick start the wider development and promotion of data verbalization I have a vision to set up the 'data verbalization lab' designed to be part of a wider strategy to democratize research dissemination, alongside the privileging of dissident knowledge both in and out of the academy (Spooner & McNinch, 2018). The idea emerged from attending the internationally renowned Chicago director's lab that brought theatre directors from around the world together for an intense exploratory period pertaining to the sharing of techniques used in directing from around the world. Creating such a space ensures there is a legacy being generated from which to guide future directors. Such is my vision for the 'data verbalization' lab.

The Data Verbalization Lab

It was out of the experience of producing 'silenced' that myself and the team I work with developed a short manifesto to assist in setting some guiding principles for those of you wanting to create 'data verbalization' stories. The data verbalization lab should:

1. … be constantly revised by 'exploring' and 'examining' the intersection of both 'research data' and 'creativity'.
2. … never become static, always creating space for further 'experimentation', 'innovation', and 'progression'.
3. …. always be critically evaluated to assess its impact/s.
4. …. work alongside other approaches and techniques with relation to the sharing, disseminating, and distributing of research data.
5. … 'improve' and 'enhance' approaches to 'presentation literacy' by recognising the power of 'storytelling'.

6.   … enable researchers and practitioners to enhance their current skills set in the following areas:

- Written and verbal communication skills.
- Interpersonal skills.
- Professional development.
- Improve culturally competent values and practice.

For anyone wanting to utilize 'data verbalization' as a method to share, disseminate, and distribute their research data there are a range of considerations that have emerged throughout its development.

1.   The 'data verbalization' method should be constantly revised by 'exploring' and 'examining' the intersection of both 'research data' and 'creativity'. The 'data verbalization' technique should never become static, always creating space for further 'experimentation', 'innovation', and 'progression'.

2.   The 'data verbalization' method should always be critically evaluated to assess its impact/s. Evaluation is therefore a key component of the 'data verbalization' technique's ongoing development.

3.   The 'data verbalization' method should work alongside other approaches and techniques with relation to the sharing, disseminating, and distributing of research data. Overall, the 'data verbalization' technique can make the overall sharing of research data a deeper and more holistic 'sensory' experience.

4.   The 'data verbalization' method aims to 'improve' and 'enhance' approaches to 'presentation literacy' by recognizing the power of 'storytelling'. By taking complex and complicated research data and make it accessible to a variety of audiences (non-academic) the outcomes can present a 'data driven story' which will enable a wider and diverse range of audiences to gain relevant insights and understandings in a simplified form. The importance here is that the 'data verbalization' technique does not only provide an opportunity to present, share, and disseminate research data, but it also gives the researcher–practitioner some additional tools from which to increase the 'researcher' identity by developing a unique selling point.

5.   To work in partnership with other vested interests in relation to building the profile of the Data Verbalization Lab. A key objective in terms of 'data verbalization's' development is to locate the technique within a global market place. The need to share, disseminate, and present research data is wider than being located within academia. Recent experiences of putting 'data verbalization' on media platforms, in community venues, and site-specific spaces, would suggest that 'data verbalization' has extended its reach, creating a variety of new opportunities.

6.   To generate original ideas and projects from which to turn PLATFORM – Data Verbalization Lab into a global brand. In the Appendices section of this report there are a several genres depicting the application of 'data verbalization'; spoken word, screenplays, theatre, etc. By undertaking an extensive

research and development phase 'data verbalization' offers the scope for the creation of more ambitious projects in partnership with potential collaborators/partners. For future development of PLATFORM – Data Verbalization Lab it is intended to explore new avenues of development: podcasting, feature films, documentaries, music, and live performances.

7. To build local, regional, national, and international networks for the exchange of knowledge and information about 'data driven' performance and to form relationships for future collaboration regarding PLATFORM – Data Verbalization Lab.

As I ponder my future I realise that a deeper philosophical question has emerged. Less about being an academic and more about 'what kind of academic do I want to be?' The future may be uncertain and full of trepidation, but I have given myself permission to pursue my intellectual freedom. A reprise of something stated earlier in the book is relevant here aimed at those who want to join me, or to those who want to stop me:

I will no longer be bound by notions of race
I will no longer be held captive or lost without trace
I will no longer be trapped by bein' told I'm not equal
I will no longer be concerned with reruns or sequels
My freedom ain't a mystery, nor wrapped up in clues
Or based on your theories, or relies on your views
It emerges from struggle, commitment, and toil
Shaped by my needs, with a passion that's loyal
My freedom is here, right now.
And I'm taking it
As I will no longer defend my right to be me

I am therefore keen to connect to others on a similar journey, who are keen to build a new constituency built of mutual support and common purpose. Who will run alongside me?

Summary

This chapter concludes the book with arguing for the need to develop more improved and appropriate methods from which to disseminate research data. It also calls for the heralding of a new era that envisions 'data verbalization' being at the vanguard of such changes. As I have argued throughout this book, there is a need to (re)present research dissemination as a counter-narratives as a way of contesting oppressive dominant research paradigms. Bell (2003) argues that future research should move beyond merely descriptive accounts of oppression. Bell further sees the need to address how multiple inequalities influence outcomes for marginalized populations.

Reflection questions

1. Where do see your role in relation to those communities seeking social justice using research as a tool for change and transformation?
2. How are you going to shape your future in relation to research dissemination?

References

Bell, D. (2003) 'Telling tales: what stories can teach us about racism', *Race, Ethnicity and Education*, 6(1): 3–28.

Bell, L.A. (2010) *Storytelling for Social Justice: Connecting Narrative and the Arts in Antiracist Teaching*, New York: Routledge.

Denzin, N.K. (2010) *The Qualitative Manifesto*, Walnut Creek, CA: Left Coast Press.

Du Bois, W.E.B. (1938) *The Souls of Black Folk*, New York: W.W. Norton.

Du Bois, W.E.B. (1978) *On Sociology and the Black Community*, Chicago, IL: University of Chicago Press.

Emirbayer, M. & Desmond, M. (2012) 'Race and reflexivity', *Ethnic and Racial Studies*, 35(4): 574–599.

Freire, P. (1970) *Pedagogy of the Oppressed*, London: Continuum.

Katz, J. (1988) *Seductions of Crime: Moral and Sensual Attraction of Doing Evil*, New York: Perseus Books.

Rich, J. (2009) *Wrong Place, Wrong Time: Trauma and Violence in the Lives of Young Black Men*, Baltimore, MD: Johns Hopkins University Press.

Serrant-Green, L. (2002) 'Black on Black: Methodological issues for black researchers working in minority ethnic communities', *Nurse Researcher*, 9(4): 30–44.

Serrant-Green, L. (2010) 'The sound of silence: A framework for researching sensitive issue or marginalised perspectives in health', *Journal of Research in Nursing*, 16(4): 347–360.

Spooner, M. & McNinch, J. (2018) *Dissident Knowledge in Higher Education*, SaskatchewanUniversity of Regina Press.

INDEX

with 47, 53, 67; impact on 11, 12, 14, 38, 45, 46, 63, 65–6, 76, 137, 147; indigenous 65, 74; inner-city 8, 28–9, 145, 146; marginalized 9, 13, 16, 46, 69, 79, 141; on-line 138; oppressed 13, 46, 145; research in 2, 8, 9, 11–12, 13, 17, 19, 20, 25, 26, 28–9, 33, 35, 47–8, 67, 68, 117, 118
community-based learning 121–3, 127, 137
community learners. *See* community-based learning
constructed self 12
contexts: community 67, 72, 121; cultural 39, 40, 71; global 3, 21, 146; intergenerational 28; intersecting 24, 39, 69; research 147; social 70, 116; social justice 26; social media 134–5; socio-historical 3; of Western scholarship 28
copyright 54, 55
counter narratives 11, 12, 13, 21, 30, 75, 142; of black performance 83; development of 14; function of 13; generation of 14; to the majoritarian narrative 21–3; need for 11; and research dissemination 140
Counter-Narrative Theatre (CNT) 49–50
counter-stories: of black men 23; individual 23; *see also* counter narratives
crime: and race 22, 78; racialization of 13, 14, 22, 23, 35, 70, 76
criminal justice 70; colonialism in 24; invisibility of blacks within 70–71; and the problems of black offenders 70–1; and race 133–4; racialization of 13, 22, 23; research in 118, 133, 134
criminology 8–9, 39, 118; cultural 33; indigenous approaches to 23–4; mainstream 23–4
critical inquiry 11, 24, 25, 36, 46, 84, 117, 142
critical pedagogy 123
Critical Race Theory (CRT) 22–3, 50, 69
cultural analysis 83
cultural competence 71–2, 118
cultural perspective 86
cultural pride 6

data dissemination 2; and 'safe' dialogue 68–9; *see also* research dissemination
data dramatization 19
data storage 55
data verbalization 30, 131–2; action learning in 73; and blended learning 121–32; and bricolage 33–41; contextualising 5–8, 14; creating and producing 43–50, 79;

through creative thought 84; engagement with 74–5; ethical considerations 54–5; future of 146–7; genesis of 2–3, 44, 50; impact of 68–9; and the inventory 52–4; pilot experience 50–2; pilot phase of 28; and the process 55; and the process of adaptation 52; and progressive research 30; and reflexive performance 86–7; and social media 133–9; teaching and learning 40; and the understanding of praxis 16–18; use in group work 30
Data Verbalization Lab 1, 147–9
data visualization 43, 80
decolonization, mental 26
deficit model 72
delegation 138
Denzin, Norman 44
dependency 76; economic 26; social 12
desistance 55–7, 79, 114
digital technology 121, 124
disbelief, suspension of 84
disintermediation 134–5
diversity 41, 51; adapting to 71; embracing 38; valuing 71
divided self 7, 8–9
documentaries 108, 149
double consciousness 6
Du Bois, W.E.B. 7, 20; as sociological bricoleur 35, 41
Durkheim, Émile 17

ebony tower 146–7
education, participatory 25–9, 31
Ellison, Ralph 20
epistemologies, multiple 39–40
ethical considerations 67; compliance with law 54; copyright 54; harm reduction 54–5; obligations to community members 54; production 54; sharing research 55; storage of data 55
ethnodrama 49–50, 87, 119, 140
ethnography 66, 75, 146; urban 35; *see also* auto-ethnography
exclusivity 2
experimentation 1, 3, 147–8
eye contact 105

facing the fear 137
father absence 78–9, 86–7
fear society 8
feature films 149
feedback 25, 28, 46, 62, 73, 77, 117
fourth wall, breaking 84
Friere, Paulo 28, 71, 145